Creative Leadership Ideas

A compilation of great ideas from great minds in great books

By Charles W. Gross, Jr.

1

Published by Charles W. Gross, Jr. through Lulu.com

ISBN 978-0-557-46516-3

Foreword

This book was written from a creative leadership
podcast series I posted in 2008 till 2010. At the time, I
was working as the Associate Executive Presbyter for
the Presbytery of Donegal. Many of the examples are
from that time period. I decided to republish this book
simply because too many of these concepts are
outstanding and timeless. Simply overlook any
outdated references to the Presbytery of Donegal. The
Presbytery continues to thrive and is doing some
wonderfully creative work. It was my pleasure to serve,
grow and learn with top-notch leaders and theologians.
It was also my pleasure to be fed by the authors of the
books I review in this book. May you grow, learn and
lead in new, creative, innovative ways.

Charlie Gross, August 2020.

Charlie's Creativity Podcast Series

January 23, 2008 to January 3, 2010.

The URL for the cast is:
https://podcasts.apple.com/us/podcast/charlies-
creativity-podcast/id272485708

This podcast series started on January 23, 2008 and continues. From 2008 till December 31, 2009, I was the Associate Executive Presbyter and the Acting Executive for the Presbytery of Donegal. As I write this book, I am again in the role of Associate Executive Presbyter and am pleased to be using my God-given administration abilities in kingdom building activities.

The following transcripts are close to the actual podcasts that are posted but are not 100% verbatim. In creating the transcripts, it was necessary to capture the ideas and the words, but often, I either missed a few phrases or could say it just a wee bit better as I write it. Also, I give the "podcast" introduction on some of the transcripts, but not all. I try to determine if the introduction adds anything to the particular written podcast. The other note is that not every podcast is transcribed. There are some that are interesting reflections, random musings, or just trivial observations that are not in this compilation. Thanks for your patience and understanding in this process. This is truly a labor of love for me. I hope that you get some value from it. I am deeply honored that you chose to download this, purchase it or just pick it up in some way.

Maybe one more note about my podcasting style. This series is not meant to be a literary masterpiece. It is written the way I talk. It is fairly simple, direct, and to the point. It's meant to be that way. Some very fine folks have asked me, after hearing me speak, if I grew up on a farm. At first I was shocked by the question, then realized that I have a definite folksy approach. I'm not making excuses for this. The only regret that I have about it is if it gets in the way of good, clear, accurate communication. Well, onward to the cast. The podcasting begins:

Meeting Strategies

(Charlie's Creativity Cast 1. January 23, 2008)

Hi! My name is Charlie Gross. I am the Associate Executive Presbyter for the Presbytery of Donegal. I am blessed to be in executive ministry and to be able to use some of the gifts God gave me in this ministry. Today I'd like to talk about some of the factors that go into the making of a great meeting. As Presbyterians, we meet a lot. It is important to us because we believe that together in prayer, discussions, and dialogue, we discover Christ's will for the greater church.

The first important factor for a great meeting is to send out an agenda about a week ahead of time. This is important so that the attendees will have an idea about what will be discussed and gives them a chance to be prepared for the meeting. It will also remind them of the meeting, the time, the location and who will be doing the devotions. Additionally, it will prompt anyone who has a follow-up action to be prepared for the meeting. This agenda can be sent out via email, fax or U.S. postal service, but it must get to the people who are expected to be there about a week ahead of time.

The second important factor is to connect the members by name, hobbies, interests and perhaps their spiritual gifts. God gives all of us very unique gifts and abilities, so it is quite important to share this information around the table so that we know who is gifted for various pieces of our work. God brings us together for his glory and for his will to be done, so we should know our unique corporate strengths and abilities and where we have gaps. This factor is also important in order to connect any late comers or new members of the group. By integrating them into the work, they are more likely to become active participants rather than idle meeting voyeurs.

The third important factor is to start the meeting on time and end the meeting on time. Along with this is the critical factor of spending time in God's Word. God speaks through the scriptures and seasons our discussions and conversations, so a good opening time of devotions and prayer is critically important. Some chairpersons use songs, hymns, prayers, readings and engage everyone in a mini worship service. In any event, prayer is essential. I have seen great meetings open in prayer that is for those around the table, those absent, and those who are ill or hurting. Another very powerful technique that I have seen used very well is for the group to split into twos and threes and spend a few minutes in prayer for one another. This helps to connect the group and bring "the Holy" into the meeting.

The fourth requirement for an effective meeting is a good note taker. It is very difficult to conduct a great meeting and also take your own notes. If you can find someone who is gifted in taking good notes and who will send them out within a few days or a week, you will do well. Notice that I said, "send them out in a few days or a week." This is quite important for those who have tasks to do. Good notes will serve as reminders for them to get them done. The notes should be sent the same way that the agenda is sent, by email, fax or postal service. The fifth factor for an effective meeting is for full involvement of the group. Everyone should be asked to speak and exchange ideas. As the meeting leader or facilitator, don't let a few people dominate the discussion and allow the others to simply sit idly by. Work to discover effective ways of involving the quieter ones. One way would be to do some brainstorming and go around asking each person for their ideas or response. Or, another way would be to get everyone to write their ideas down on a piece of paper or 3 by 5 card. By writing ideas down, it allows for sharing ideas without the possibility of being put down for having a dumb idea. You could experiment with other techniques of getting the entire group involved in some way.

The final requirement covered in this podcast is a good summary of the meeting with action steps. In other words, who will do what, by when. After you determine the next meeting date, time and location, then go over what was decided. Name the actions to be taken and the people responsible for doing each one. This summary technique helps to etch these actions into their brains and also helps the note taker to get these accurately recorded. You might find that those responsible will pick up a pen or pencil and make themselves a note as a reminder. Send the folks off with a prayer that captures the spirit of the meeting, maybe ties in a word from the devotion and gives them courage and enthusiasm for the work ahead. In this way, you will have a great meeting and they will call you a great meeting leader. May God Richly bless you and yours and of course your ministry.

Advanced Meeting Strategies

(Charlie's Creativity Cast 2. January 29, 2008)

Today I'd like to cover some advanced factors to consider for effective meetings. I have recently found some very interesting ways of scheduling meetings, conducting meetings via conference calls, and a few other tips that will serve to advance our work. Let's get right into the meat of this.

Scheduling meetings, appointments or conference calls for a large number of people can be a very daunting task. I found a way to make this a very smooth process. It is based on the requirement that those to be invited to the event have email and internet access. At this point, I have not been able to streamline the process for those lacking these essential tools. I am using a website at www.doodle.com for scheduling. This website makes scheduling very easy. Here is how it works. Go to the website, www.doodle.com. Click on "schedule a poll." Give the event a name and a brief description.

Enter your name and email address in the optional box. Click next and you will see a calendar pop up. You then select the potential dates for the meeting or event. Click next and you will be given the option of entering a number of times in each of the dates selected. Once you are done, hit save or finish and you are done with this step. You could either have doodle send this link out or you can choose to do it. I have always chosen to send it out myself. Doodle will send you two web links. One is your administrative options link. Do not send this one out. The other is the participant link. This is the link that should be placed in an email to all of those who are being asked to come to the event that you are trying to schedule. Oh, don't forget to go to the link yourself and enter all of the good dates and times and then click save. Once your invitees click on the link, they are sent to the doodle website and they can then enter the dates and times that are good for them. This website then creates a running spreadsheet of the best date and time for your event. This is an incredibly useful and powerful tool for your use. I have been using it for a few months and love it.

The second advanced tool to discuss is free conference calling. I found a number of options here at websites called www.freeconference.com and www.freeconferencecall.com . If you spend some time in these websites, you will discover free ways of getting a good conference call number and an access code. You then simply schedule your conference call with the doodle tool above, give everyone the conference calling number to use and the access code and voila, you have just set up a virtual meeting. It is that easy. This meeting option saves lots of time, gasoline, and hassles. There are many options available in these websites such as recording the call, 800 number toll free calls, etc. Check out the range of possibilities.

Another advanced meeting technique that I learned from serving on a pastor nominating committee is to end the meeting with a series of questions like this: What of this meeting should be communicated to others? How will this be communicated? (in other words, what will be the medium – pulpit announcement, newsletter article, bulletin announcement, email, letter, etc.) Who will do this communication? We found this technique extremely useful in keeping the congregation informed in our work. Perhaps you know this – it is extremely hard to OVER communicate. By asking these excellent questions at the end of every meeting, we were able to provide outstanding communication and keep our process moving in a healthy way.

The last advanced meeting tool that I will cover today is called, Mutual Invitation. This is an outstanding technique developed and used by Eric H. F. Law for a community Bible study process. According to the PCUSA Peacemaking website, the chair or the meeting leader speaks first. Upon finishing, the facilitator invites the next person to speak. That person has the opportunity to speak to the issue, to pass, or to pass just for the moment. After speaking or making the choice to pass, this person has the opportunity to invite the next person to speak. This process continues until everyone has had the opportunity to speak. It is vital to note the use of the word – invite. Participants are given an invitation to speak. This technique is useful in balancing and moderating power. If you choose me or direct me to speak, you have taken away my power. By inviting one to speak, you give them a choice to speak or pass. In that way you are sharing power with one another. Each participant shares power equally. They have the power to speak, pass, and invite others to speak. You may ask questions of the speaker for clarification only. This model is very powerful for sharing power and for listening to one another. We listen and are listened to. These are simple gifts that we too rarely experience. These are gifts that we need to share with one another as we seek to live abundantly in God's creation. I hope that you can use some of these advanced tools in your life and ministry. May God Richly bless you and yours!

Two Brains, Four Eyes and More

(Charlie's Creativity Cast 3. February 6, 2008)

This cast is called, "Two Brains, Four Eyes, and More." This cast is about collaborating with others for wisdom. Last Friday, I had a doctor's appointment to look at a skin blemish to make sure that is was not some form of skin cancer. I accepted an early appointment with a nurse practitioner. She examined it closely, asked a few questions and then rendered a verdict. There was nothing to be concerned about. Then I reminded her that I was just making sure that it wasn't any form of melanoma. She thought for a second and then said, "Let me get a doctor in here for another opinion." Another brain and two more eyes will help to be doubly sure. Well, in a few minutes a doctor appeared. He examined it, asked a few more questions and then rendered the same conclusion as the nurse. He re-assured me that it was nothing to worry about. Two brains and four eyes were helpful to me. This process raised my confidence level. The nurse just winked at me when the doctor rendered the same conclusion. I knew what she was thinking.

Another recent example in my work takes this illustration a bit further. I was asked if I needed more help in my executive ministry work. After considering this, praying about it and reflecting on my needs, I concluded that I didn't need more paid help, but I could use more wisdom and counsel. I suggested that I needed a "master mind" group or an advisory council to meet once a month for an hour via conference call to help guide my priorities and help me to know what should **not** be a priority. I used the doodle.com website to determine a meeting date and time and then used free conference.com to put together a conference call with the top officers of our organization. They were eager to join this process of providing guidance. It's a great feeling to have a lively dialogue on my work and where the top priorities should be. Another benefit is hearing some affirmations of some of my gifts. Hearing these named is exhilarating and helpful. One more benefit to the organization is the checks and balances and accountability it shows for my work. In this example I used six brains in a sixty-minute discussion for greater clarity in my work. I'm going to keep looking for ways to bring brains together to solve problems, answer questions and raise the bar in ministry in the Presbytery of Donegal. Hey, have a great creative week.

Leadership.

(Charlie's Creativity Cast 4 - Leadership. February 10, 2008)

I have a passion for leadership. I study leadership. I read about it. I try to exhibit leadership traits in my work. Today's cast will be a very condensed look at Warren Bennis' book titled, "On Becoming a Leader." (Bennis, 2003) The first edition was published in 1989, but was updated in 2003.

Ideas are the engines of leadership today. Leaders innovate. They look for new ideas. They have an ability to play with new ideas. Leaders are creative and imaginative. They look for and foster ways of developing their creative and imaginative abilities. They are constantly trying to shape and mold reality into new value, new realities, new innovations. Leaders get excited about ideas and innovation. So, ideas are critically important to leaders. They constantly scan the horizon for new ideas. Ideas are the clay, the putty, the bricks and mortar for leaders.

Leaders are also collaborators. Leaders try to bring creative people and ideas together in new and different ways. They seek to foster learning in these collaborative "get togethers." As they bring people and ideas together, leaders try to connect the dots. They look for the larger good, the big picture. They look for new ideas that emerge, the themes that seem to be bubbling up in the system. Leaders work diligently to bring people together from across the organization. In this way, they seek to break down the walls, the functional silos, and the stove pipes for the greater synergy and effectiveness of the organization. Leaders also pay a lot of attention to people. They encourage people. They build up people. They inspire people and bring the best out of people. Leaders listen to people, mentor and coach people. Leaders listen to the problems that people are experiencing and seek to equip people to find their own solutions.

Leaders are communicators. They get people together. They communicate and over communicate. They give their people the information necessary to do a good job and then give feedback, encouragement and inspiration for constant improvement. They reward people when they get work done. They are encouragers. They have a way of creating community to get things done.

Leaders are visionary. They are long term thinkers. They constantly swim against the fast-flowing stream of short-term thinking. Often the culture provides enormous pressures to meet the weekly, monthly and quarterly deadlines to the detriment of the long view. Leaders resist this and spend time thinking strategically.

Leaders also trust their inner voice. They trust their guts and instincts. They are long range thinkers. They define the mission. They communicate the mission. They are clear about the mission and spend time communicating the mission. In fact, they beat the drum so often and so loudly that people are clear about the mission and understand their individual part. Leaders then reward people for their accomplishments in achieving the mission.

Another characteristic of good leaders is character. Character is difficult to teach. You can teach leadership skills in various courses, but it is difficult to teach character and integrity. Good leaders have character and integrity. Leaders continually do the right thing. They look for the right thing to do and do it. Leaders have passion, enthusiasm and are positive thinkers.

Leaders have integrity. They honor their commitments. They do what they say they are going to do. Leaders are there when they need to be. They show up. Leaders accept responsibility. They take on various roles, jobs and tasks and follow through. They are straight forward and communicate constantly. They keep talking about what they see as current reality and how they see the preferred future reality.

Leaders are communicators extraordinaire. They communicate, communicate, communicate. They tell everyone everything and then tell them in a different way. They are also perseverant and imaginative. Leaders are encouragers, equippers, and coaches. They have the solid character of integrity.

Leaders also have adaptive capacity. They have the ability to face reality. They accept responsibility in the face of reality. They work to break down walls, silos and functional areas and bring people together. They can affect change and transformation. They have great communication skills. They communicate reality. They tell what could be and their version of future reality. They learn by leading and handling crises. They face reality and look for ways to collaborate with people and ideas. They communicate what they see. Leaders have the ability to create flexible environments.

Leaders are learners. They are curious and experimental. They learn from reality and situations. They constantly try to learn from the situations around them. Leaders know themselves. Leaders reflect on their experiences. They don't just act and move on. They reflect and learn from the experiences. Leaders are innovative learners.

Leaders are made from experience. They reflect on experiences and learn from them. They are formed in learning. They learn in the fray and by getting in the trenches with their people.

I hope that these nuggets are helpful or at least pique your interest enough to explore them deeper. To capture these ideas in their entirety, I highly recommend Warren Bennis' book, "On Becoming a Leader." (Bennis, 2003)

The Leadership Engine and the Presbytery of Donegal

(Charlie's Creativity Cast 5. February 19, 2008)

This week's cast intersects Noel Tichy's excellent work called The Leadership Engine with our work in the Presbytery of Donegal. (Tichy, 1997) Dr. Tichy's premise is that an organization needs leaders who have a teachable point of view and they build capacity by teaching others to be leaders who teach others and so forth. The core of the book deals with many great leaders in business and it stresses the generation of ideas, the absolute necessity of strong values, that positive, enthusiastic contagious energy is essential, and that leaders should have edge (which is the ability to face reality head on and respond). Finally, Tichy tells us that great leaders tie all of this together in a great story. They paint a powerful descriptive picture of the organization in the future. Everyone can see their role and place in this.

The Presbytery of Donegal is in transition. For many years we were operating with two full time executives. For the last year and a half, we've been functioning with just one. During this time a committee decided to hire a transition consultant and put together a dynamic team of servants to work on discerning who we are a presbytery and how we should function and be structured. It's an exciting time to be serving in this presbytery. Many elders and Ministers of Word and Sacrament are working diligently in many areas of ministry and service.

Here's how I see us putting into practice the ideas in Dr. Tichy's book. We are designing our presbytery meetings with ample time to have numerous presentations on how to raise the bar in ministry. These presentations cover topics like – assessing spiritual gifts, using mediation team resources, communication practices in congregations, telling faith stories, making mission a focus, how to do extended communion, etc. These presentations generate enthusiasm and more ideas for ministry.

Elders and Minister gain value from these presentations and then seek to stretch their own ministry.

The area of firm values is being stressed in a number of ways. The presbytery council put together a very solid statement of values in the 1990s. These are included on every meeting docket. We read them as a presbytery in a recent meeting. The transition team and transition consultant are asking for our values in their "holy conversations." Each of the administrative commissions is striving to resolve differences in the most Christ-like way possible. We are trying hard to walk the talk and live out our values.

In the positive energy area, the Presbytery of Donegal is steeped in a rich tradition of mission giving and mission mindedness. We celebrate this, enjoy leaning into mission giving and making a difference in the world in the name of Jesus Christ. We also are creating lots of positive energy through the use of a dynamic electronic newsletter, called the Presbytery of Donegal eNews. This newsletter is published biweekly and contains tons of good information, video and audio links, schedules, mission news and opportunities and information from around the presbytery. We've received many high accolades for this informational, energy producing initiative.

Having an edge is what we're working hard at developing. The definition of having edge in Dr. Tichy's book is the ability to face reality and respond to it creatively but with the ability to make the hard decisions. The presbytery loves to err on the side of grace and bends and changes and has found ways of skirting hard decisions. One note about this. The finance committee and Council believe that we soon may be forced to make some hard decisions. In light of this, the presbytery Council is now in a prayerful season regarding mission priorities. They are in dialogue, scripture and prayer on how to lead the presbytery. I believe that we are in a good place. What better way to face reality and creatively respond with hard decisions than by bathing ourselves in prayer and discerning dialogue?

Finally, the Presbytery of Donegal has been writing a wonderfully faithful story of following Jesus Christ into the world for 275 years. It's a story of sisters and brothers praying, worshiping, serving and giving. It's a story of drawing others into this caring community and the story continues. The story that we're writing now is one of deepening spirituality and expanded learning opportunities. We are trying to stretch and grow and build capacity to face whatever the future holds. We are writing a story of building more Christ-like leadership capacity. It's an exciting time to be in the Presbytery of Donegal and I am privileged to be part of this story.

I highly recommend the book, "The Leadership Engine." There is even a workbook built-in it to assist in your leadership development.

The Importance of Story

(Charlie's Creativity Cast 6. February 27, 2008)

One of the most interesting and captivating books I've read lately is titled, "A Whole New Mind, Why right-brainers will rule the future," by Daniel H. Pink. I found this 2005 Riverbend book on a table at BJ's wholesale club. It was like striking oil or finding gold in this big box store. (Pink, 2005)

One of the key concepts that jumped out at me was the importance of story. According to Daniel Pink, stories are how we remember. He says, "Narrative imaging or story is the fundamental instrument of thought. Making an impact in the world today requires the art of putting words, pictures, and emotions together in a memorable way – a story. Facts and data are cheap. With instant information at our fingertips through comprehensive databases and search engines, what matters is the ability to place facts in context and to deliver them with emotional

31

impact. The vehicle that carries this information with emotional impact is story."

When our savior, Jesus, walked the earth, he was known as a great teacher and prophet and made a lasting impact on the crowds by telling relevant, memorable stories.

Daniel Pink offers a fascinating example of choosing a bottle of nine- or ten-dollar wine. The first two bottles have labels that are descriptive with fancy wine adjectives. Lots of facts and data. The third bottle told a story. Here is that story as quoted from page 111 of the book, *"The idea for this wine comes from two brothers, Erik and Alex Bartholomaus. They wanted to sell a great wine, sourced by Alex, labeled with Erik's art, in a non-serious way for a good cause. Their goal was to pay homage to their late mother who suffered an untimely death due to cancer… Alex and Erik will donate 50 cents from the sale of each bottle of Big Tattoo Red to Hospice of Northern Virginia and/or various cancer research funds in the*

*name of Liliana S. Bartholomaus. Thanks to your
support we have donated approximately $75,000 from
the sales of our first release, and hopefully much
more in the future. Alex and Erik thank you for
purchasing a bottle of Big Tattoo Red in honor of their
mother.* (Pink, 2005)" Guess which wine he bought.
Stories that draw us in, that paint a picture of a
brighter future, and tug at our emotional heart strings
help us to find meaning, significance and purpose.

This brilliant book suggests an exercise to
sharpen our creative story writing ability. It suggests
a format called a mini-saga. A mini-saga is a
complete story with a beginning, a middle and an end
using fifty words exactly, no more, no less.

My first attempt is a story about my experience
as a chaplain at Camp Donegal in southern York
County Pennsylvania. Listen to my mini-saga and
then write your own. "A crackling fire with smoke
wafting into the night sky sets the stage for deep
meaning. Friends sharing stories of faith and life from
stumps. Sunny, smiling faces softly singing shape a

prayer, no, a dialogue, no a life transforming relationship with the living, Lord Jesus Christ! That's Camp Donegal." (exactly 50 words)

Creating Energy and Life

(Charlie's Creativity Cast 8. March 12, 2008)

This week may be a brief cast, but I trust it will be powerful, energizing and life giving. I want to talk about a few traits that may re-invigorate you and transform your life and attitude. Here they are:

Walk faster with more focus and direction. Speed up your actions and you will feel more confident, more alive and more in control. You will feel this way and others will perceive you in that way. You will be seen as one on a mission. One who gets things done. One who is in charge and one who can be trusted. So, walk and move faster is your first assignment.

The next trait is about language. ALWAYS be positive in your greetings. In fact, be over the top in greetings. When asked, "How are you?" your answer should be something like - Awesome! Fantastic! Super! Fabulous! I'm doing Great! I am richly blessed! You get the idea. You may not feel quite that way when you say it, but after you say it, you'll start to feel better. You will start programming your body, mind and spirit to be awesome, fantastic, super and fabulous. I challenge you to try this out for yourself. Start moving faster and programming your feelings by stating how incredible you are and there are good chances that you will start to feel that way. There is a Japanese psychotherapy that uses this principle. In a nutshell, it states that you can't control your feelings. Feelings come and go as they please. But, what you do control is your behavior. So, if you know your purpose in life or even your purpose for the moment and are controlling your behavior toward that purpose, then your feelings may eventually change for the better. This change may occur because you see what you are accomplishing. Of course, if feelings are not controllable then your feelings may not change so you will still feel terrible, but you'll have accomplished your purpose anyway. The point that I am trying to make is that if you act enthusiastically and act like you're on a mission and talk like you're on

top of the world, then pretty soon you will be. Give it
a try and see if it works for you.

Leadership Development Best Practices

(Charlie's Creativity Cast 10. April 10, 2008)

Hi! This is Charlie Gross with another podcast on creative leadership topics. This week's cast is connecting some dots from an article by Josh Bersin in the February 2008 edition of Chief Learning Officer (Bersin, 2008) – available at www.clomedia.com, actions proposed by the Synod of the Trinity and my goals for the Presbytery of Donegal.

Here we go. I'll frame it around the article by Josh Bersin. The article is titled, "Leadership Development in 2008," on page 18. Josh tells us that leadership development is one of the fastest growing areas of corporate training. The Synod of the Trinity discovered this same desire in a majority of their presbyteries. Then in a series of table talks in January and February 2008, the single most requested initiative was for leadership development. On May 5th 2008, there will be a Synod meeting to discuss and vote on making leadership development

38

the single major thrust for the Synod. I believe that we are on target in this important area.

Josh Bersin framed his article around the six best practices in successful leadership development initiatives that were uncovered in two years of research. The first and most important one is the strong executive engagement. This means that a top level commitment is given, is real, and that the top leaders work toward coaching, teaching, and mentoring other leaders. It means that time, money and resources are used to raise the bar. The Synod will be voting to make this a priority. The Presbytery of Donegal has made this a goal priority area for their work.

The second-best practice is "tailored leadership competencies." This speaks to the necessity of identifying those competencies that are important in your line of work. For pastors and elders, I can envision identifying those factors that contribute to building relationships, sharing faith and hope, and finding ways of lovingly holding folks' accountable for follow through and results. We can explore best practices in our field and then train to this level.

The third best practice is "alignment with business strategies." The work that you are doing determines your focus. When you are directing a mission trip or leading a team you are focusing on a different set of factors than when you are developing a session or planning a presbytery or synod strategy. As you focus on the bigger picture, your role becomes one of designing good systems and processes and getting the right people in the right tasks. That is far easier to say than do. This is very tough work. Just today, I heard a senior pastor say that he is working hard to get gifted people in ministry roles and not simply filling slots with volunteers. This is aligning talents with business strategy.

The fourth best practice is to target all levels of leadership. This is such an important, all-encompassing initiative, that every person should be in a progressive developmental program. Our challenge is to be more intentional in identifying appropriate experiences for all people. This leads to the fifth best practice.

The fifth best practice is to apply a comprehensive and ongoing approach to leadership development. Our programs should include 360-degree assessments, case studies, podcasts, poster sessions, books, webinars, seminars and workshops. The Presbytery of Donegal is becoming rather progressive in this area, but much more can be done.

The final best practice identified by Bersin and Associates is to integrate with talent management. This translates into a good leadership assessment program to help identify talented leaders and then get them placed in the right experiences. These are very challenging concepts and are even more difficult to apply in non-profit settings. But, in my mind, success is to at least try.

Balancing Power in Meetings

(Charlie's Creativity Cast 11. April 18, 2008)

Hi! I'm Charlie Gross. Thanks for downloading this podcast. The other casts are available at www.charliegross.com. Today I'd like to talk about balancing power in your meetings. We generally spend lots of hours working collaboratively in teams, groups, staffs and committees. Balancing the various voices in this work is important. Everyone on our team has valuable skills, abilities and knowledge. Highlighting and listening to all of this knowledge is your role as a leader. Doing this well is a real leadership skill.

One tool that can be used in your meetings or gatherings to get at all the inputs is the tool called, "mutual invitation." It is a tool that is a very simple process of having the meeting participants invite others to express their opinions or pass. By paying attention to who has spoken or passed and who hasn't, you interject an added dimension of caring for one another. And, your caring shows that you are including everyone.

Some groups have used a "talking stick" in this way. They will hand the talking stick to a meeting member and that hands the power of voice to the stick holder. The person has the right to speak or pass, after which they hand the stick to another and invite that person to speak or pass.

In mutual invitation, a stick is not used, but a simple invitation is used instead. The only requirement in this is that the team members must know the others' names or be able to read their name tags. The following is an example of how this technique may be used.

"Ok, friends, for our next item of business, it is very important that we get everyone involved in the decision process. We will use the tool called, "mutual invitation." To use this, I will invite someone to speak first and then they will invite another person and we will continue this until everyone has had a chance to speak. When you are invited to speak, you may express yourself and then invite another or you may pass up your chance to speak and then simply invite another.

This technique can work very well, so I invite you to give it a try. You will get better at its use through practice.

Reviewing the book, "Presence."

(Charlie's Creativity Cast 14. May 17, 2008)

This cast is a short review of the book, Presence, An exploration of profound change in people, organization, and society, by Peter Senge, C. Otto Scharmer, Joseph Jaworski, and Betty Sue Flowers. (Senge, 2004) This was originally published by the Society for Organization Learning in March 2004. The authors have come to believe that the core capacity needed to access future is "presence." They define this as deep listening, being open beyond one's preconception and historical ways of making sense. It results in a "letting come," consciously participating in a larger field of change.

The authors name a chapter, "seeing our seeing." In this chapter, the importance of suspending our own judgments and prejudice emerges. It is the capacity to develop new eyes and fresh senses that examine our own biases, experiences and opinions.

William Isaacs from Massachusetts Institute of Technology (MIT) claims that most of us see only two ways to dialogue. First, defend why we think the way we think, or two, say nothing. Isaacs points out a third possibility which is to suspend one's view. So, rather than defend your view, you would respond with, "That is not the way I see it. My view is….(and you would explain your view). Here is what has led me to see things this way. What has led you to see things differently?" by practicing this way of interacting, and doing it sincerely, it can open up a deeper and richer dialogue. Real learning can occur.

The next chapter of this thought-provoking book deals with seeing from the whole. This is the capacity to redirect our awareness toward the generative process that lies behind what we see. To see deeper into the system. The authors use an automotive engineering example that shows how different teams were working to optimize their own areas to the detriments of the whole project. They wanted to look good or creative or brilliant in their own specialty. When the light bulb finally went on, the solution revolved around the two-letter word, "we." When blaming, finger pointing and use of "they" went away and the concept of "we" showed up, people's awareness and capabilities change. By a redirection of focus to the larger purpose, we get a more holistic view of the generative underlying process.

Until people start to see their own handprint on problems, fundamental change rarely occurs. Well, I've only scratched the surface of this book and topic, but it's quite a morsel to chew on. I highly recommend the book and will explore a bit more of it in the next podcast.

Reviewing the Theory of U

(Charlie's Creativity Cast 15. May 22, 2008)

Welcome to creativity cast number 15. This cast is a continuation on the book by Peter Senge, C. Otto Scharmer, Joseph Jaworski, and Betty Sue Flowers called, Presence: An Exploration of Profound Change in People, Organizations, and Society. We're going to focus some time on Otto Scharmer's concept of the giant U shape. This image of the U is a model that Otto has been developing to examine and explain different levels of perception and change. In simplistic terms, the process entails three major stages or elements. The first is located at the top left of the U and it is "observe, observe, observe." Become one with the world. The second is at the bottom of the U and is "retreat and reflect." Allow the inner knowing to emerge. The third is on the upper right of the U and is "act swiftly with a natural flow." These three elements are referred to as sensing, presencing, and realizing. Sensing, as was mentioned, involves careful attention and observation. Really seeing what reality is presenting. The difficulty in this step is not to see through the same old filters and prejudices that you've formed through life experiences. Trying to bracket or step out of old sensing and seeing patterns is very hard work. I remember an example from Japanese management literature as they train a new automotive engineer in factory processes. They draw a circle on the floor near an assembly line and tell the engineer to stay in the circle for the day and observe the assembly line and associated processes. It's focused attention. It's a discipline of really seeing. Presencing is being awakened to a whole new reality. It's like seeing a new possible future as a whole new exciting story. It is being drawn into that future and being present to a larger space, an expanded self. It's also said to be looking back at the present from the future.

I have to admit, these are very difficult abstract concepts. But, they put language around concept and help us talk about deep issues of change.

49

The final concept of this triad is Realizing. Realizing is moving into the new reality that is formed out of the sensing and presencing. It is a flow of new connections, new relationships, new orientations. It is like a new symphony being played with just the right timing, melodies, and instruments. When the string section blends with the keyboard and the brass merges melodiously with the percussion section, stirring music emerges. This is a picture of realizing change.

A core principle in the theory of the U has to do with the relationship between us as observers and actors, and the world in which we operate. The key question is, "What does it mean to act in the world and not on the world?" The U theory suggests a stance of "co creation" between the individual and the larger world. Later in the book, it expands on this same concept by claiming that leadership in the future will not be provided simply by individuals but by groups, institutions, communities and networks. The

U theory shows us that the future can emerge from within a group.

For me, personally, I find this theory fascinating and fitting, for I have never felt like a wise, expert or traditional leader. I continue to rely on the chorus of highly talented voices to sing just the right anthem for our time.

Reviewing the book, Masterful Coaching

(Charlie's Creativity Cast 16. May 27, 2008)

Welcome to my sixteenth creativity podcast. This cast is a short glimpse at coaching. I will be taking a very fast tour through a few chapters of Robert Hargrove's revised edition of Masterful Coaching. This edition was published in 2003 by John Wiley & Sons. (Hargrove, 2003)

One of Mr. Hargrove's first assertions caught my attention. He asserts that masterful coaching is based on inspiring people to realize an impossible future that they can passionately engage in. Wow! What a statement. It is packed with energy, a pull toward the hopeful future, and full of positive emotion. The author says that a masterful coach inspires, empowers, and enables people to live deeply in the future while at the same time acting boldly in the present. Additionally, a masterful coach makes a strong commitment to the coachee. This takes the form of an opening like this: "It is my intention that this conversation make a difference for you." The total focus of the coach is on the coachee. The coach listens fully, attentively, with every sense employed. The coach tests assumptions and observations by asking direct questions. If the coach feels like something is missing or that some non-verbal cues are communicating, he or she will be honest and forthright about what is being sensed. The coach will ask to validate this feeling or go deeper for more. All of this is intended to be helpful for the coachee. Coaches give their coachees the great gift of "real presence," and the gift of really being there for them. Coaches listen from a commitment to unearth what the coachee passionately cares about and then links this into the extraordinary future they want to create. One of the Mr. Hargrove's coaches puts it this way, "I actually listen from a commitment that people are going to leave the conversation feeling freed up, clear, and empowered to act... My point of view is that people possess within themselves the ability to resolve their upsets, do their own thinking, discover

their own answers and their own path forward."
(Hargrove, 2003)

Masterful coaches don't just listen to what people are saying about what happened, but listen for the underlying beliefs, assumptions, and interpretations that are made.

Coaches help people reframe their story. The author says that the way we tell our story about who we are or what happens to us is not just based on facts and events, but on how we interpret these facts and events. Masterful coaching involves helping people surface, question, and redefine their stories when the current story is called into question or breaks down.

So basically, coaching is "other focused." It is a supportive relationship which is designed to create a space and a framework for the coachee to do the hard work. Coaching is a playful way of drawing out the ideas, stories, experiences and expertise of the one being coached.

This is just a very small morsel from an outstanding book. I hope that you look deeper into coaching because we really need a larger number of encouragers in our lives. Well, I know that I do!

Reviewing the book, Co-Active Coaching
(Charlie's Creativity Cast 17. June 10, 2008)

This cast contains more reflections on coaching. I've just finished a great book by Whitworth, Kimsey-House, and Sandahl, titled, Co-Active Coaching. It was published by Davies-Black Publishing in 2007. (Whitworth, 2007)

This cast will be a brief synopsis of the first chapter. It lays the foundation for the co-active coaching model. Coaching focuses totally on what the client wants. This may be one of the hardest concepts to grasp. As a coach, you probably have lots of knowledge, life experiences, expertise and maybe even best practices in the field. So based on that, your tendency is to lead the client in that way or to find ways to offer your advice. But, to coach well, you are totally listening to the client, paying attention to their wishes, their fears, their desires, their inner voices, and their emotions. In fact, the term, "co-active" means that the coach and the client are both active collaborators in the relationship. The coach's role is to ask questions and invite discovery. The coach's job is to be curious, to pull the agenda from the client and to challenge the client to go deeper or further for resources and innovations. The clients' role in this relationship is to stay engaged, be actively challenged, and work hard at achieving their goals. The co-active coaching model is rather simple. At the center is the client's agenda. This agenda has three components: the client's fulfillment, the clients' life balance, and the process of life. Fulfillment is very personal and again is defined totally be the client. What makes them happy or satisfied? What does success look like to the client? The client's life balance is being intentional in devoting time, attention, and resources to family, work and self. The processes of life are dealt with in this coaching model as shifting priorities, shifting seasons of life, and different ways of handling the information that comes our way. With the client at the center of this model in terms of fulfillment, balance and process, we surround them with five contexts.

Those five are listening, intuition, curiosity, forward and deepen, and self-management. Listening is one of the most important pieces of coaching. Listening intensely and deeply to the client's words, stories and emotions and getting behind these. The coach listens at many levels simultaneously to hear where clients are in their process, to hear where they are out of balance, and to hear their progress on their journey of fulfillment.

The context of intuition is hard to describe. It remains in the background because many people don't trust it. According to the authors, however, this is one of the most powerful tools of coaching. After listening intently and actively, your intuition will sometimes give you hints about the situation that are not obvious. The context of curiosity is a powerful, fundamental tenet of coaching. The coach's main role is to ask questions and guide the discovery process. This context is open, inviting, spacious, and playful. It also has a way of breaking down walls and barriers and teaches clients to be more inquisitive.

The fourth context is called "forward and deepen." This is all about moving forward in life, getting things done, and learning as you go. It's asking the client about a commitment to action. To getting to the place they want to go.

Finally, the self-management context is about the coach bracketing his or her own agenda and focusing on the client. It's about not taking things too personally. Setting aside your preferences, biases, pride and ego.

Reviewing "The Art of Possibility"

(Charlie's Creativity Cast 18. July 4, 2008)

This podcast was inspired by Zander and Zander's book, "The Art of Possibility." (Zander & Zander, 2000) Ben Zander is the conductor of the Boston Philharmonic Orchestra and is a teacher and speaker. Rosamund Zander is a family therapist and runs accomplishment groups. They form a synergistic couple in "transformational processes." They seek to assist us, not just in making incremental improvements, but to make large scale shifts in improving our lives and professions. The practices that I will cover today are: It's all invented, universe of possibility, giving an A, and being a contributor.

The first practice is called, "It's all invented." It is a response to the way our minds work. We take in the data and details of the world through our senses and then the mind goes to work to connect the dots and make sense of it. We seek rational explanations from within the bounded set of assumptions. Our minds are quick to think within the box. There is a cute little example of this where there is a set of nine dots in the shape of a square and the object is to connect all nine dots with just four straight lines without lifting the pencil from the paper. The feat can only be done by drawing the lines outside the box. So, to help unbind the mind, here's the first practice. Ask yourself, "What assumptions am I making that I am not aware that I'm making?" When you have the answer to that question, ask, "What might I now invent that I haven't yet invented, that would give me other choices?" Then you invent spaces and other possibilities for your work. You expand the box. You step out of narrow assumptions and invent greater opportunities.

The second practice tries to counter the narrow world of measurement. Basically, we live and move and think in terms of measurements and scarcities of time, money, power, resources and strengths. We measure everything and compare and contrast things to describe them and discuss them. This world implies a certain size of the pie. A world that has finite resources. This type of world demands thinking around the zero-sum concept, which means, if I have more then someone has less. To stretch ourselves and our thinking into the world of possibility, let's imagine a world that is infinite, generative and abundant. A world unimpeded by scarcity and limited resources. In this world, you believe that by giving more away you do not deplete your wealth. That your customers are unlimited, that the good you can do is unbounded. You operate by believing that resources are likely to come to you in greater abundance when you are generous and inclusive and engage people in your passion for life. This new thinking and operating will take you past the world of measurement and into greater possibility. To help take yourself to this new level, first ask yourself, "How are my thoughts and actions in this moment reflections of the measurement world?" This question asks for a deeper analysis of your thoughts. The Zanders' encourage you to continually ask this question in order to go deeper in your self-analysis. In this way, you delve into your own assumptions that shape your thinking and your life.

The next practice is called, "Giving an A." It's all about bringing out the full potential of folks. It's about stretching people by giving them an 'A' rather than a 'B' or 'C' and then asking them to come up to this level of performance. Here is a creative example of this technique. In one class taught by Ben Zander, he says this, "each student in this class will get an A for the course, but there is one requirement. Sometime in the next two weeks you will write me a letter dated next May which begins with the words, "Dear Mr. Zander, I got an 'A' because ....." In this letter you are to tell me in as much detail as you can, the story of what will have happened to you by next May that is in line with this extraordinary grade. The letter is written in the past tense and explains who you have become and the accomplishments achieved. Mr. Zander received some of the most inspirational letters in this exercise and even wonderful follow-up letters. This exercise seems to be in line with the halo effect or the fact that people will often step up to our expectations of them – so expect the best!

The next practice is called, "Being a contributor." The question to ask yourself each day is, "How will I be a contribution today?" Then, you declare yourself to be a contribution and throw yourself into life as someone who makes a difference, accepting that you may not understand how or why. Well, we've only covered the first half of the book, but it's enough to work on for now. Until we meet again work on asking:

1. What assumptions am I making that I'm not aware that I'm making that gives me what I see?
2. What might I now invent that I haven't invented that would give me other choices?
3. How are my thoughts and actions in this moment, reflections of the measurement world?
4. How will I be a contribution today?

Finally, look for ways to give others A's. Expect the best out of others and let them know!

Part Two of the Review of "The Art of Possibility"
(Charlie's Creativity Cast 19. July 15, 2008)

This is the second of a two-part series on the book titled, "The Art of Possibility: Transforming your Professional and Personal life," by Rosamund Stone Zander and Benjamin Zander. (Zander & Zander, 2000) We will continue in briefly describing the practices the Zanders' recommend to transform your personal and professional life. The practice of "Leading from any chair" is one based on a symphony example and means that from your current position in life, you have way more influence and game changing capacity than you realize. When you perform your job with excellence, go above and beyond the call, and lead when it's appropriate, you become a standard bearer. The military has a term for this concept of "everyone being a potential leader." It is called, "commander's intent." This concept means that if the commander's objectives and goals are accurately communicated and understood across the entire field of soldiers, these can be achieved even in the face of suffering a personnel loss because the overall objective is understood. Everyone becomes a leader when necessary. Everyone becomes the standard bearer.

Another practice highlighted in this book is "The Way Things Are." It is the concept that we can be at peace when we accept things we cannot change. Not in a resigned, giving up, way, but in a proactive sense of being present to the way things are – even including our feelings about it. It is an active acceptance and it is an alertness to what is or might be possible in the present situation. The Zanders point out that by being alert to the present, you are poised to speak possibility into the future. You can avoid the downward spiral of negative thinking and look for the half-full glass rather than the half-empty one.

Bill Hybels' Opening Remarks at the 2008 Leadership Summit

(Charlie's Creativity Cast 21. August 9, 2008)

This podcast will summarize Bill Hybels' opening comments from the 2008 Leadership Summit. This summit was beamed to a host of cities across North America. I attended the summit at the Lancaster County Bible Church (LCBC – now called Lives Changed By Christ). At this summit, LCBC won the year's Courageous Leadership Award for their work in Africa.

Bill's reflections on leadership started this way. Leaders lead by decisions. Big decisions, like, "let's feed 10,000 starving people in Zimbabwe. Tough decisions like how to balance a budget in tight economic times by letting people go from the staff. Leaders lead by decisions they make every day. Therefore, an important area of reflection and study is this, "how do leaders make decisions?" Bill Hybels suggests the following process: 1. Does the Bible speak to it? 2. What do smart advisors say? 3. What have I learned from the pain of past decisions? The gain of past decisions? And my experiences in decision making? And finally, 4. What is the Holy Spirit prompting me to do? Could I make a trial or test decision and walk around with it? Live with it for a while and see if I have peace with it? Leaders have to be decision makers. They can't avoid making decisions, for in that sense, they aren't truly leading.

Bill next recommends creating your own axioms for your own leadership style. He published a book called, AXIOM with some seventy of his own axioms. He highlighted a few from his book, but I'll cover just one.   It is, "create motion for motion's sake." In other words, create energy, enthusiasm, power and action. Create action every day. The physical law of entropy says that energy dissipates over time. The leader's job is to keep people moving. Keep the vision and mission alive. One of the beneficial images that was painted in this year's summit was that of a bucket with holes in the bottom.

Bill used this image to say that "vision leaks." People lose sight of the big picture, the big vision, the reason for mission and ministry. So, the leader's job is to keep people, resources, and energy focused on the vision. Leaders need to find creative, zany, life giving ways to keep energy high, keep people connected and engaged and keep them pointed toward the larger purpose. Leaders use stories to do this. Leaders use facts and figures to do this. Leaders use images, videos, initiatives, retreats, and multi-sensory means of communication to do this. Leaders use exaggeration and emotion to capture the hearts and minds of people to work toward the vision.

Surviving Information Overload

(Charlie's Creativity Cast 23. August 27, 2008)

This is cast number 23. Today I want to spend a few minutes on an incredibly important topic. Surviving Information overload. If you're even a little bit like me, you are interested in lots of subjects and ideas and the information, emails, newsletters, books, seminars, and discussions come like a flood. We are deluged with information. Our task is to somehow stay afloat. Our task is to manage the information or organize ourselves so that we can handle it intelligently. In a bookstore at the Reading Outlets, I happened upon one called, "Surviving Information Overload," by Kevin A. Miller. (Miller, 2004) Kevin is Vice President of Christianity Today International, editor-at-large of Leadership Journal and the executive editor for Preaching Today.com. This book is literally stuffed with great ideas for handling the tsunami of information. I'll share only a few of these.

One of the first ideas listed is to define your own key information areas. What are the main subjects that people around me depend on me to know? What does my boss, or spouse, or family rely on me to know? What information is cataloged or is contained in easily accessed resources? What are my key strengths and areas of interest?

Next, hone this list to a short list. Now you can concentrate your information gathering and filter what you read, listen to, and watch to raise your knowledge level in these focused areas. This strategy will help you to start managing information. Once you've selected key focus areas, you're getting set to capture ideas and learning in these areas. Creative "idea" capturing comes in the form of: tearing out magazine articles, filing emails in special key folders, using notecards, journals, diaries, Word documents, book shelves, tape recorders, digital recorders, phone messages to your answering machine or secretary, white boards or butcher paper in the office, power point or post-it notes. You could record your ideas and images with a digital camera or video camera. By creating a focused set of key learning areas and then establishing a way of cataloging and organizing your notebooks, cards, electronic files, you will have improved your system of managing data and knowledge.

The book spends some time with excellent email managing strategies through the use of filters and rules, but I can't cover that here. I recommend getting some help with creating rules, filters and blocks to handle your email. Then the recommendation is to only check your email a couple of times a day, rather than "all the time," like I seem to do.

The one huge take away for me was how Kevin emphasized taking one or two actions out of every book read or workshop or conference attended. Rather than taking copious notes from an experience and then just putting them on a shelf, he suggests taking only a couple of notes about behavior changes that he is committed to and then changing. He also

suggests using a simple matrix for meetings that
captures what action is to take place, who will do it,
and when will it be done. He urges us to not allow a
meeting to move on until commitments for action are
made. Well, by writing this short synopsis of the first
part of this excellent book, I've taken actions with
what I've read. I hope this spurs you on to new
creative ideas.

Reviewing "The 5 Dysfunctions of a Team"
(Charlie's Creativity Cast 25.   October 18, 2008)

This is cast number 25. Today, I'd like to summarize the model from Patrick Lencioni's 2002 book called, "The 5 Dysfunctions of a Team." (Lencioni, 2002) This book is an excellent, fast read with some incredibly useful tips on creating a productive, results-generating team. Let's jump right in. The author uses a fable style approach to cover the five main points and then summarizes these points in the last pages. He uses a triangle to depict these building blocks to show that building a foundation is very important.

The first dysfunction of a team is, "the absence of trust." When team members come together, there is often a "closed," guarded approach or attitude. Team members don't automatically open up and become vulnerable to one another. So, the first critical task of a team leader is to build personal relationships. Intentional team building, exploring ways of being real and human with one another is very important. It takes some time but can start to generate a much more effective team. Tools often used are, "off sites," inventories like the Myers Briggs Type Indicator, and personal history discussions.

The second dysfunction is a fear of conflict. This fear arises from the lack of trust, but it is stifling because real issues, ideas, and opportunities are not discussed in an open and honest manner. Teams that experience this fear will have boring, "surface issue" meetings. They won't drill down to the critical issues which may be controversial and emotion-producing. Team members will just play it safe. To counter this dysfunction, a team leader first has to build trust, but then will actively look for the "buried" controversial issues and constantly remind members that conflict is ok, as long as it has to do with the facts and issues. The team leader will guide the team away from interpersonal attacks and toward healthy energy producing conflict.

The third dysfunction is "lack of commitment." This problem arises when team members will not support the team decision after a healthy debate and analysis. It can also arise from a team member who is trying to promote herself or department over the good of the team. The important points here are that an effective team will commit to a team decision even if consensus is not reached AND even if there is a level of uncertainty about the decision. If there is trust and good interaction and debate, an effective team needs to commit to the decision and go forward.

The fourth dysfunction is "avoidance of accountability." When a team has a direction and a goal that they commit to, it is necessary for them to help hold one another accountable for their efforts. If team members let one another slide, the effectiveness decreases rapidly. To counter this dysfunction, it is helpful to have published goals and standards and regular progress reviews. These tools help build accountability and transparency into the system.

The final, fifth dysfunction is "inattention to results." When a team has clear, focused goals and objectives, it is obviously critical to keep the main thing the main thing and only reward those behaviors and actions that contribute to achieving the announced goals. Dysfunctional teams will wander off track and confuse activity with success or completely lose sight of their primary target or purpose. A team leader will relentlessly focus the team and will reward and recognize positive results.

There you have it. By building trust, promoting healthy conflict, gaining real commitment, establishing accountability, and staying focused on results, you will be a great team leader. I hope this brief synopsis, whets your appetite for this excellent book and also helps you to become an outstanding team leader.

Our Language and our assumptions

(Charlie's Creativity Cast 26. November 8, 2008)

Welcome to my 26th podcast on creativity, learning and leadership. Today's cast deals with our use of language and our assumptions. I'm taking these concepts from a very powerful book titled, "How the Way we Talk Can Change the Way We Work: Seven Languages for Transformation," by Robert Kegan and Lisa Laskow Lahey. This work was published in 2001. (Kegan, 2001)

This book presents a new technology of using language to create and sustain change. A premise of the book is that changes in groups are accomplished by individual behavior change. And, individuals don't change their behavior without changes in their interpretations and underlying meanings. So this book presents seven languages that help us examine and change our underlying meanings. I will try to focus on and make clear the first four languages which serve to build an engine for change.

The first language is called 'from complaint to commitment.' This is the language and strategy to turn whining, complaining, and negative talk into positive energy. Often, we see the problems in our work, but this language asks us to see the passion behind the complaining. The example the authors use for this includes complaining about a workplace where no one talks to each other. Everyone talks about others and bad-mouths everyone. Using the language of commitment, you could say, "I am committed to more open and direct communication at work" or "I am committed to honesty, integrity, and straight talk." This commitment is written down in the first of four columns. It represents an unrealized goal or desire.

Now for the second language, which will fill the second column of our engine. This is the language of personal responsibility. The basic question to ask is this – "Based on my commitment, that I just wrote down in the first column, what am I doing or not doing that is keeping me from realizing my commitment?"

This can be powerful language to find your personal role in not achieving your goal. It could be a small part or large part, but somewhere, there will be actions or behaviors that you could or should do or actions or behaviors that you should refrain from doing that are blocking your commitment attainment.

Now that you have columns completed with your commitment, and what you are doing or not doing that inhibits it, we dive into the third language called, "competing commitments." By looking at what you are doing or not doing regarding fulfilling your commitment, what does this suggest to you about a 'competing commitment?' Let me give an example. If you are committed to running a very efficient office, but in your second column, write that what you don't do is "correct employees when they make a mistake," your competing commitment may be "avoiding conflict," or "being liked." This language helps you examine your baser traits or your more fundamental character. The authors say that these three columns cause our immune system to come into view. It shows how we live with commitments (column one) that are in tension with competing commitments (column three); both being true.

So now that we see how we live with our own tensions that keep us in equilibrium, let's examine the fourth language. This is the language of "the big assumption." This is the language we'll use to disrupt the equilibrium and help us change.

The authors, Kegan and Lahey, have done voluminous research in education and change and have come to the conviction that "most people are carrying on about as bravely and effectively as they can within the world of their assumptive designs." So, here is where the fun starts in discerning "our big assumptions." To do this, we will examine our third column, the one where you have listed your competing commitments. Let's say that your competing commitment is "to avoid conflict at all costs." To determine your "big assumption," you ask a question that negates your column three answer. You answer the question, "I assume that if I did not avoid conflict at all costs, then… (and you complete this). Finally, you ask, "How would I feel then?"

The power of this model lies in playing with your 'big assumption,' observing ourselves in relation to the big assumption, actively looking for experiences that cast doubts on our big assumption, exploring the history of our big assumption, and finally designing safe tests of our big assumption. This work is all about objectively observing, testing and refining our assumptions. If we can be more precise in our assumptions, and give them appropriate qualifiers, we are in a better position to change and grow.

I hope that this short narrative encourages you to buy the book and dig deeper into the power of the seven languages for transformation.

A Sense of Urgency by John Kotter

(Charlie's Creativity Cast 27. November 24, 2008)

Welcome to my 27th creativity podcast. I focus mainly on leadership ideas but delve into other creative ideas in his series. Today's cast will try to highlight the main concepts in John Kotter's book, "A Sense of Urgency." (Kotter, 2008) Dr. Kotter is the Konosuke Matsushita Professor of Leadership Emeritus at Harvard Business School and is a world renown authority on leadership and change. He has recently published, Leading Change, The Heart of Change, and Our Iceberg is Melting.

In the book, A Sense of Urgency, Dr. Kotter deals with the first critical step of a successful transformation. This step, in a nutshell, is creating and sustaining a sense of urgency that is as high as possible among as many people as possible. This first step in the change process is so important, that it can make or break an organization. Organizations often will develop a homeostasis or comfortable balance of routines. There will be complacency and a settled standard operating procedure that is rather unresponsive to change, culture or customer needs. Responding appropriately and timely requires energy, time, and attention. Moving an organization from complacency, the routine, the way things are always done requires leadership initiative.

Dr. Kotter emphasizes the role of leadership in creating a sense of urgency through head knowledge and heart knowledge. It is not enough to show the facts and data that cry for change, leaders must paint the picture and tell the stories that impact the emotions, the heart. Leaders are effective story tellers. Leaders are relentless story tellers. Leaders will find a variety of ways to not only tug at the heart's emotions through stories but will also live out those stories and dramatize the point. Leaders live out the change that they are creating by going there first.

I once heard that Ray Kroc, the founder of MacDonalds, emphasized cleanliness of one of his restaurant's properties by taking off his suit coat, rolling up his white shirt sleeves and picking up trash around the parking lot. The store manager got the point. Ray demonstrated his priority.

So, according to Dr. Kotter, leaders create emotionally compelling experiences. They also behave every day in every way with the real urgency they are trying to create. Leaders live their message. They also live in a highly visible way, so they must be a visually consistent message to those whom they lead. To use a worn cliché, they must walk the talk.

Another tactic that leaders use to create real heart-head urgency is to look for potential opportunity and the positive side of every crisis. Napolean Hill, who wrote the classic, "Think and Grow Rich," wrote that whenever he got any bad news he would say, "that's good," and then would work to find out what could be good about the bad news. This trait takes real courage, creativity, and energetic leadership.

The final tactic for creating a sense of urgency is "confronting the naysayers" and moving them either out of the organization or into positions of minimal influence. This tactic helps with the laser like focus of the change. As you lead change, gather supporters, use heart and head information, live the message and look for opportunities, it is vital to align all of these factors toward the positive. For this reason, you may have to neutralize the negative voice and forces.

Well, there you have the important four tactics for creating a sense of urgency. If you are a leader at any level, I recommend that you read Dr. Kotter's books and then start walking the talk, telling your emotion producing story and living out the positive message. In doing so, you will create real urgency and you will be on the way toward making a positive difference in the world.

Re-Imagine! by Tom Peters

(Charlie's Creativity Cast 28.   December 6, 2008)

This cast is a brief visit with Tom Peters as I draw great inspiration for my work in the church from his 2003 book called, Re-Imagine! (Peters, 2006) Tom Peters has been called the "father of the post-modern corporation" by the Los Angeles Times. He has spent his career in business and was first published in 1982 with his classic, "In Search of Excellence." I draw inspiration from Tom by the passion and emotion he packs into his writing! He challenges bureaucrats and institutional thinkers with hope, possibility and large, grandiose dreams. He says, "I don't believe in initiatives. I believe in Full Scale Assaults on enormous opportunities!" That catches my attention. That gets my blood flowing. That preaches! I believe in an all-powerful, almighty, sovereign God. I believe in thinking really big and going for it in big projects, so Tom Peters knocks me out of my rut and routine.

Tom, in his flashy, zany way puts a mirror up to us and says, "what do you see?" People who are just getting by? People who are doing normal, run of the mill work? People who aren't being challenged or are using just a fraction of their brain power? Tom Peters' off the wall style reminds me of a pastor friend of mine, Jeff Lampl. Jeff's first call to ministry was to a small, struggling church called, New London Presbyterian Church. Jeff tried for seven to eight years to find the right "transformative fix." He read every book, went to every seminar and workshop and was relentless in his pursuit. Finally, he hit on Rick Warren's "Purpose Driven Church" model and New London took off! It now worships over five hundred a Sunday and averages three hundred for their Friday night youth program. The factor that I see in operation is Jeff's untiring, relentless efforts to pursue being relevant, vital, faithful, and centered in the heart of God. Jeff is essentially doing for the body of Christ, what Tom Peters is urging for business leaders. Pursue with a passion anything that might make a powerful positive impact for customers. Never sit back and coast, relying on tradition or the way it's always been done. Try new things without fear of failure. Peters even suggests that by failing fast, you learn fast and by failing big, you are more able to learn and succeed big.

Tom Peters' trademark is a large red exclamation point. He's passionate and a fanatic! He rants and raves about people and businesses that don't get it, that coast along, doing mediocre work, not caring about their impact or their quality or what type of experience their customers have.

In the economy of 2008 and beyond, you have to read this book. We all have to zealously search for ways of using our God-given gifts to bless others, add value for people and begin new ministries and missions that are self-sustaining. We have to cobble together the resources, ideas, and people to try new things, create new services, invent new products, and craft new experiences. Coasting is not an option.

I believe that, as Christians, we have to re-ignite our passion for Jesus Christ and tell others our stories of how and why we are different because Christ lives in us. In fact, I believe that Jesus would urge us to be zany, passionate, committed and on-fire rather than ho-hum lovers of God.

Well, I've talked myself into going for it. So thank you, Tom Peters! Thank-you for reminding me that I'm blessed, gifted and made by God to be creative and innovating in worshiping and glorifying God and serving God's people.

Hey, until next time, have a super-charged creative week!

Benefits of using a coach

(Charlie's Creativity Cast 29. December 16, 2008)

This is episode number 29. Today's cast is an attempt to explain the benefits of using one of our coaches to help strengthen your ministry or build your ministry team. The Presbytery of Donegal takes its role of equipping the saints for ministry very seriously, so we have been training a small number of coaches to help our churches build up the body of Christ. We are delighted to add this tool to our toolbox, for we believe that this option will be very useful if you are feeling stuck or just can't seem to gain traction.

Ok, so what would a coach do for you and what are the benefits? A coach would meet with you or you and your team to build a relationship and clarify the main desires or issues. The coach would listen closely and carefully to 'hone in' on the goals, targets, objectives, and purposes of your ministry or ministry team. This would involve a time of listening and questioning to get a precise understanding.

The coach would then help to assess and analyze the situation and start to uncover the skills, ideas, talents and resources of the team. The coach might use a number of tools, checklists, inventories or methods to fully assess the situation.

The next piece of work that would be done is to determine what else needs to be learned or discovered. After drilling down into the core issue, assessing the reality of the situation and the skills and resources that surround you, the coach would then help you uncover gaps in your knowledge and additional areas for learning. This work is done through careful listening and focused questions.

Finally, the coach would enter a phase of the work characterized by motivating the team for the work. This phase is about identifying the next steps to be taken, when they will be accomplished and who will do them. The coach will then help hold the team accountable to their work. The model just described has the acronym CALM. C for clarify, A for assess, L for learning, and M for motivate.

There are a number of benefits for using a coach. Coaches are trained in listening carefully, asking key clarifying questions, reframing issues, and drawing out the potential of your ministry team members. Coaches can be the ones who ask the hard questions and can help to foster an atmosphere of accountability.

**The Importance of Conversation. Inspired by
Margaret Wheatley**

(Charlie's Creativity Cast 30.   December 27, 2008)

My name is Charlie Gross and you've honored
me by downloading this podcast. This has been a
labor of love in 2008 and this thirtieth cast closes out
the year.

This cast is centered on an incredibly powerful
principle I've discovered in Margaret Wheatley's book
titled, "Turning to One Another, Simple Conversations
to Restore Hope to the Future," (Copyright 2002 and
2009) (Wheatley, 2009)

I recently downloaded and listened to this book
from the iTunes audiobook area. Dr. Wheatley's
other works, and I recommend all of them, can be
found at www.margaretwheatley.com . I believe that
you'll be enriched and blessed by her works, writing
and thinking.

Well, to dive into this current work, "Turning to
One Another," one of the key premises is that "There

is no power for change more powerful than a community discovering what it cares about." The primary way that a community discovers what is truly important is through conversation. Real conversation, listening intently to one another, hearing the passion, the emotion, the stories, the meaning and the experiences. Striving and struggling to be authentic, present and real for one another, speaking from the heart.

Dr. Wheatley gives examples of movements, institutions and organizations that were begun because two or three concerned people gathered around a kitchen table and chatted about their concerns. Lives are changed, saved and improved when people share their ideas and creative thinking. Laws are enacted for the common good when concerned citizens give voice to their opinions.

So how does this happen? Well, it can certainly happen by chance as people share with one another around tables or over fences, but Dr. Wheatley advocates for intentional conversation groups. To give hope for a brighter, more positive future, we are encouraged to proactively start conversations with small groups. Dr. Wheatley gives a number of conversation starters, but you can craft your own around 'what is important or interesting.' A few of Dr. Wheatley's starters are: "Who else should be here? What is my faith in the future? Where does it come from? Our future comes from our actions, values, and beliefs. If we want a new future, we simple act to change now and our future will change." Another starter is: "What do I believe about others? Can we build trust? Can we find human goodness? Can we treat people as humans rather than as objects or machines?" Or, try this one, "When have I experienced good listening? Can we tell people our stories, build relationships and be heard? Being heard, really heard with all of our emotions and quirks is healing and life-giving!" finally, consider this one, "Am I willing to reclaim time to think? Can I slow down and be more reflective?"

Well, those are just a few ideas for starting your own conversation groups. You can check out others at www.turningtooneanother.net .

In my work for the Presbytery of Donegal, I will be looking for new ways of proactively starting conversations with passionate lovers of Jesus Christ. I personally am very hopeful for the future. My prayer is that, as you grow in your creativity, and share it with others, you will experience God's extravagant blessings!

Reviewing "Influencer – The Power to Change Anything"

(Charlie's Creativity Cast 31.   January 10, 2009)

This is cast number thirty-one. It's the first in 2009 and is all about the best- selling book titled, "Influencer – The Power to Change Anything," by Patterson, Grenny, Maxfield, McMillan and Switzler. (Patterson, Grenny, Maxfield, McMillan, & Switzler, 2008)

The power and promise of this book is that, and I quote, "almost all the profound, persuasive, and persistent problems we face in our lives, our companies, and our world can be solved. They can be solved because these problems don't require solutions that defy the laws of nature, they require people to act differently." Let me emphasize this, "they require people to act differently." It's about a behavior change, and we'll soon learn that it's about key behaviors or vital behaviors that have a significant impact on the outcomes.

One early example of a key behavior was the ten/ten scanning at YMCA pools. It was discovered that if a lifeguard stands in a specific spot and scans their section of the pool every ten seconds and then offers assistance to anyone in trouble within ten seconds, drowning rates drop by two-thirds. That is a critical behavior change.

So, the first task in influencing change is determining what you want to change and then put this in behavioral terms. What behavior needs to change? The second part is to find the vital few behaviors. What are the key critical behaviors that will make a great difference? An interesting example was given concerning counselors observing a married couple discussing a subject in which they disagree. In fifteen minutes of observation, the expert counselor could predict with ninety percent accuracy how likely the couple would be together in five years. They have discovered the key phrases, attitudes and behaviors used by successful and unsuccessful couples. It's about observation and key behaviors. According to the authors, we can learn by observing the best. By closely watching experts perform, we can learn the important behaviors that make a large difference in results.

I've recently learned a very powerful communication technique from my friend Ken Smith. I noticed that upon wrapping up a conversation, Ken takes a few moments to summarize our decisions and actions to be taken. What a great gift as a communicator.

This book quotes a number of social learning scientists but says that the father of this science is Dr. Albert Bandura from Stanford. According to Dr. Bandura, if you want to alter behaviors, you have to help others answer two questions: Is it worth it? And can they do it? He goes on to say that verbal reasoning rarely carries the day. People need to see the change and experience the change. And, if they can't personally experience the change, they need a vicarious experience through someone else. They need to watch someone change, hear about the change, feel the change personally, through stories, testimonies, videos, etc.

The book offers a number of real examples of foreign radio shows and television shows that modeled behavior for their communities that ultimately made positive differences in family relationships, in real social behavior. Perhaps it's obvious, but modeled behavior and vicarious experiences are powerful in influencing change.

Until next week, ponder the changes you'd like to make in your own life or the life of your church or organization. Also, ponder what those changes look like in behavioral terms. If you can, go watch an exemplar performer model the behavior and note the vital few key behaviors that make the difference.

The next cast will be on the second half of the book where we will unpack a very powerful model of influencers.

Continuing to Review, Influencers – The Power to Change Anything

(Charlie's Creativity Cast 32. January 14, 2009)

Today's cast is part two of two on the book, Influencers – The Power to Change Anything. (Patterson, Grenny, Maxfield, McMillan, & Switzler, 2008) In part one, we focused on finding key behavior changes to make. This cast will briefly describe the model of six powerful influencers. According to the authors, two primary mental maps determine behavior change. Those mental maps are motivation and ability. Those maps are a result of the two questions, "Will it be worth it?" (corresponds to motivation) and "Am I able to do it?" (corresponds to ability). So motivation and ability are the first two domains of the model. The next factors in the model are the personal, social, and structural. So now the model consists of a three row, two column matrix. The columns are motivation and ability. The rows are personal, social and structural. Therefore, the six

103

elements of this model are: 1. Personal motivation or making the undesirable, desirable; 2. Personal ability – surpassing your own limits; 3. Social motivation – harnessing peer pressure; 4. Social ability – finding the strength in numbers; 5. Structural motivation – designing rewards and demanding accountability; and 6. Structural ability – changing the environment to make behavior change possible. I'll try to give an example for each of these elements, but I definitely recommend the book to help you flush out more great concepts.

So, here we go with an example for the six elements of the model.

The first row is the personal row. Personal motivation and personal ability. For personal motivation, you'll want to get someone to try out the new behavior, turn it into a game, appeal to their moral values, or find a way to connect with intrinsic rewards. When people are accountable to themselves, they are motivated.

The second personal element is ability. This element boils down to practicing perfect behavior, getting good feedback, reflecting on behavior and repeating practice until you get it. According to the authors, in simple skills such as typing, driving, golf, and tennis, we reach our highest level of achievement after about fifty hours of practice. Fifty hours of deliberate, focused practice with clear, specific, repeatable action steps with immediate feedback is key.

The next row in our model is the social element. Social motivation and social ability. Social motivation translates to peer pressure or peer support. Dr. Everett Rogers discovered that the majority of people will not change or behave in a new way until their well-respected opinion leaders change. This forms the basis for testimonials from trusted sources. And, it's helpful to have about 5% of your target population here. Another important aspect is being held accountable by peers. If the norm is not one of excellence and peers let you underperform, lasting positive change will not stick. Everyone has to be in the game of mutual accountability.

In the row of social ability, we think of power in numbers. This category builds capacity through creating networks of teams who support one another, fill gaps in skills, teach one another, cover for blind spots, create camaraderie, and provide a high level of creativity. It's team building to the extreme.

Our final row is structural motivation and ability. Structural motivation is associated with "designing rewards and demanding accountability." Rewards are well designed when they come quickly after a vital behavior. Even small incentives that are immediately linked to vital behaviors yield great results. An important note of caution here – reward behaviors, not results or outcomes. Sometimes outcomes will hide inappropriate behaviors.

Finally, structural ability. This means – change the environment. Two or three examples here from the book (Patterson, Grenny, Maxfield, McMillan, & Switzler, 2008) include the "broken window theory" of crime by New York City's criminologist, George Kelling. This theory holds that where there is a blighted neighborhood of abandoned buildings and broken windows, crime goes up. The broken windows show that nobody cares. Kelling taught the New York Transit Authority to sweat the small stuff – eliminate litter, eliminate graffiti and the like and the crime will go down. Our lesson here is to pay attention to an excellent environment.

Another principle in structural ability is to make the invisible, visible. With the use of signs, pictures, graphics and images of expected behavior and established standards, you make behavior easier to achieve and much easier to receive feedback. You see, clear information vitally affects behavior. With some rather elementary changes in our environment, we can enhance our overall ability.

This completes the powerful model offered by Patterson, Grenny, Maxfield, McMillan and Switzler and gives us a lot to work on as we seek to positively change the world.

Total Leadership by Stewart Friedman

(Charlie's Creativity Cast 33. January 24, 2009)

My passion is studying leadership, reflecting on new theories and trying to apply these new theories in my work. My latest read is Stewart Friedman's 2008 book titled, "Total Leadership," published by Harvard Business Press. (Friedman, 2008)

Dr. Friedman has spent many years at the Wharton School and is the founding director of the Wharton School's Leadership Program and its Work/Life Integration Project. The book offers an outstanding program of leadership integration across four domains of life – work, home, community, and self. Dr. Friedman says, "I have come to see that the point of the Total Leadership program is to create what I now call, 'four-way wins,' better results at work, at home, in the community, and for yourself." (Friedman, 2008)

This program stands on a three-legged stool of authenticity, integrity and creativity. Authentic leaders articulate a vision – a compelling image of an achievable future. They use this image, this story, to inspire people around them, to create a preferred future. These authentic leaders are constant learners and teachers. They are great observers and reflective and know their priorities, their strengths and their weaknesses. Finally, they are great listeners and hold themselves and others accountable for pursuing valued goals. Great total leaders are holistic and they act with integrity. These effective leaders balance their domains of life through intentional processes of communication. They nurture social networks and partnerships that are catalysts for creating meaningful results. This leg of the stool helps to bring complete integrity to identifying your most important people - your stakeholders. Once your stakeholders are identified, it is critical that you determine what their expectations are of you and it is equally important that you name your expectations of them.

Leaders with integrity will use various forms of communications to validate performance and behavior expectations at work and on the home front. Leaders gain clarity about how they are performing and check with their stakeholders on what is expected of them.

The third leg of the stool is being innovative and creative. This leg has to do with the fact that effective leaders constantly explore new ways of achieving goals. They are firmly results driven while remaining flexible in their choices of how, when, and where things get done.

The next chapters of the book use exercises to help direct some focused thinking, writing and reflecting. These processes are clarifying what is important to you and to your stakeholders. Dr. Friedman suggests the use of the narrative story to draw out important life events, heroes and values. By writing a clear story about significant life events, reflecting in writing on their meaning and then writing about your "leadership vision" for the future, you are bringing into focus those things that are important to you.

Two other vital take-aways from this book are the stakeholder clarification sheet and conducting experiments to improve performance in all areas of your life. In the stakeholder clarification sheet, you identify your key stakeholders. Who do you work for, live with, and interact with in the work, home and community dimensions? Once you name these individuals, schedule conversations with them to determine their specific expectations of you. Once you have clear expectations, evaluate yourself against these. How well are you doing?

While you're in these conversations, you can let your stakeholders know what you need from them. What input, knowledge or resources do you need to perform well? This is your chance to be clear with them. By spending time in these areas, you will be able to determine your performance gaps. Once you know your performance gaps, you will be able to design experiments to more perfectly meet the expectations of your stakeholders. According to Dr. Friedman, a total leadership experiment is a planned change, something that is a do-able stretch. It is deliberately aimed at making life demonstrably better in all four domains – work, home, community and self. By creatively designing experiments, scoring yourself, and evaluating your successes and failures, you will learn how to be a true total leader in the four important areas of life.

I whole heartily recommend the book as a powerful tool to improve your life, your performance and your leadership abilities.

Review of Crucial Conversations

(Charlie's Creativity Cast 34. February 6, 2009)

This cast is a very quick review of some great concepts found in the New York Times best seller – Crucial Conversations – Tools for talking when stakes are high. This is a 2002 book by Patterson, Grenny, McMillan and Switzler. (Patterson, Grenny, Maxfield, McMillan, & Switzler, Crucial Conversations - Tools for talking when stakes are high, 2002) I heartily recommend the read. It is packed full of excellent tools. I'll share just a few. One of the first key points is this and I quote, "When it comes to risky controversial and emotional conversations, skilled people find a way to get all relevant information (from themselves and others) out into the open." The authors call this, 'filling the pool of shared meaning.' By working hard to ensure a safe environment for sharing and speaking up, the data, information and knowledge grows. Better decisions are made. When there is an atmosphere of intimidation or superiority or other venues for squashing input, the pool of shared meaning is depleted and poorer decisions are made. The authors cite examples of medical accidents occurring in hospitals when doctors are not open to questions or concerns by other staff members. In my previous career in aviation, I studied numerous accidents that were directly attributed to a cockpit atmosphere of intimidation. In these situations, crew members do not speak up when their input is critical to safety of flight. So, the first important lesson is to create an atmosphere of trust and safety for all to contribute. This will fill the pool with shared meaning.

The second tool is what the authors call, "searching for the elusive AND." Here's how it works. In a potentially conflictive situation, "clarify what you really want." Form the precise language of your heart's desire. The book example says, "What I want is for my husband to be more reliable. I'm tired of being let down by him when he makes a commitment that I depend on." Second, 'clarify what you don't want.' Again, be precise in naming the undesirable outcomes. This will help with shaping the "and" question. The book uses this example. "What I don't want is to have a useless and heated conversation that creates bad feelings and doesn't lead to change." Third and finally, present your brain with a complex problem formed by stating what you want and don't want as a question. The book example is, "How can I have a candid conversation with my husband about being dependable and avoid creating bad feelings or wasting our time?" The authors suggest that by presenting our brains a more complex question than an 'either/or' question, it causes deeper thinking and reflection and fosters more creative solutions.

The final tool that we'll cover is "mastering our stories." This tool is useful as we analyze our experiences, emotions and responses. Also, it grows out of the premise that 'others don't make you mad. You make you mad.' You and only you. Here's how it works. There are four parts. First, you experience an event by seeing and or hearing the event. Second, you tell yourself a story to help understand it or make sense of it. Third, your story causes your emotions or feelings about the event. Fourth, you now act or respond based on your feelings. To recap this, you see or hear an event, you tell yourself a story, you feel a certain way and then you respond. If you want to change your emotions, feelings or behavior, tell yourself a different story. You may need to slow down the pace and consider another interpretation of your experience, but this is key! Don't victimize yourself or sell yourself short by use of stories. If you take active, positive control of the stories you tell yourself, you will be on the road to creating new emotions and new healthier behaviors.

My hope is that you can slow down, reflect on how to put some of these tools into place, create better dialogue and thrive in crucial conversations. For more of the tool chest, definitely buy the book.

Reviewing Crucial Confrontations

(Charlie's Creativity Cast 35. February 17, 2009)

This cast is a very quick review of some great concepts found in the 2005 book by Patterson, Grenny, McMillan and Switzler called, Crucial Confrontations – Tools for resolving broken promises, violated expectations and bad behavior. (Patterson, Grenny, Maxfield, McMillan, & Switzler, Crucial Confrontations - Tools for resolving broken promises, violated expectations and bad behavior, 2005) This cast may sound a bit like my thirty-fourth podcast because that one was on 'crucial conversations' by the same authors and uses their same model. I have to tell you that I have found these books very helpful in giving me new ways to see situations, new tools to assess dilemmas and new insights into my own conversations and conflict style. I recommend that you buy the book and spend time reflecting on and unpacking these nuggets.

Let me open up this tool shed for you. The first great tool helps you decide what issue to confront. The acronym for this tool is CPR. It stands for "content, pattern and relationship." Here is how it works. When someone violates and expectation, misbehaves, causes you grief and needs corrected, you call them on the carpet with CONTENT. (the C of CPR). To effectively address this, you recite the content of the person's behavior. You say how the behavior was inappropriate and name the consequences it caused. In using 'content,' you are addressing a single event. An example could be, "you missed a very important deadline delivering your report, you did not notify me that you needed more time and this embarrassed me."

The next time that this same problem occurs, you will address the P of CPR, the pattern that is occurring. Your focus will not be on the missed deadline. Your focus will be on the repetitive nature. You might say, "This is the second time that you missed this deadline without notifying me. You had

118

assured me that it would not happen again. This is a pattern that makes me wonder if I can rely on you."

Finally, if the same problem continues, you focus on the R of CPR, which stands for relationship. You may say something like, "Your continued behavior of missing deadlines is causing a strain on our relationship. I don't believe that I can trust your word in keeping commitments." When you get to this step, it is again important to make the key issue and confrontation about the relationship. If you skip back to the content or the pattern, you are losing ground and not keeping the main issue at the foreground. So, our first tool to use in assessing issues to confront is CPR. Content, Pattern, Relationship.

The second tool for the same purpose is to unbundle the consequences of poor behavior and the intentions. Here is what the authors mean. They make the case that the behavior is not the problem (in our case, the missed deadline and no warning to this), it is actually the consequences of this that is the problem. In other words, what pain or grief or money or missed opportunity did this cause? What was the consequence of the bad behavior? By examining the consequences, you may be able to note and discuss the real damage that is being caused to the organization, the relationship or to others who count on you. Focus the issue around the consequences.

Secondly, this tool asks you to examine or discuss the intentions of the person. Do they perform or not perform with an intent to make you look bad? Do they intend to overachieve, better themselves, or work in a creative way? By truly discovering their overall purpose and intentions, we can narrow down the issue or issues to confront. The authors cite a few examples of supervisors assuming intents, telling themselves stories of possible hostile intentions and then acting on these.

This presents an interesting dilemma. You either have to uncover true intent or confront your perceived or assumed intent. The authors suggest that you share your observations and then check your conclusions with the other. Let me give an example.

You could say, "Helen, I'm not sure I have this right, so I'd like to check my observations and conclusions. You then share them and end by saying, "This is what it looks like to me. Am I missing something?"

By trusting your observations and conclusions and being tentative, you are asking for input and feedback and not putting your whole foot in your mouth without a dialogue.

So there you have the second tool – examining consequences and intents. I hope this has been helpful in your work. For more tools, grab a copy of this book and hone your skills in confrontation.

For a complete list of my other podcasts, check the link on my homepage – www.charliegross.com Until next time, have a great, creative week! May God Bless You!

Excellent Coaching Advice from David Clutterbuck

(Charlie's Creativity Cast 36. February 17, 2009)

I'm fascinated by the study of leadership, excellence, productivity and encouragement. I hope that your work, ministry or service are enhanced by today's podcast. This cast is a brief extract from David Clutterbuck's excellent 2007 book titled, "Coaching the Team at Work." (Clutterbuck, 2007) I highly recommend the read for it is packed full of coaching questions and approaches to bring out the best from your own work or service situation. My concentration will be on what Mr. Clutterbuck calls the solution-focused coaching scenario. He claims that the solutions-focused coach will work **with** a team or task force to help them achieve their goals or purpose. The coach will use an appreciative inquiry approach or methodology toward this end. In simple terms, this means that the coach will focus on solutions, build on successes, energies and passions of the team, highlight their available resources and skills, and help them to discover new perspectives and frames of reference. This tact is basically sound in that you are building on strengths and building on your team's gifts. The tension and warning flag that I raise comes as I respond to the author's statement, "If something works, do more of it." In today's fast changing environment, nothing fails like success. Or, as Einstein once said, "We can't solve our current problems with the same thinking that created them." So, my response is to use the skills, passions, and energies of your team, but find ways to take these in new, creative directions and to new levels through reframing the issues. Distill the nuggets of what works, but "what works today," may not be the solution for tomorrow.

The author claims that the solutions focused coach helps the team extract its successful behaviors and processes by questions such as (and I'll paraphrase them, though they are the authors' thinking and style): "What positive moments were

there in our period of stagnation? Where was the
energy? What happened that made these positive
moments different? What can we learn from these
positive moments that would help us tackle the
current issue differently? If you had already resolved
the problem, what would you and others have done?
What would the action steps have looked like as
replay our success?"

Another model and set of questions might be
as follows: The author suggests that we place our
team on a continuum scale from one to ten. Ten
represents the ideal state. One represents the
opposite. After placing the team on a number from
one to ten, you would ask, "How did you get to this
point on the scale? What efforts, skills, actions and
resources were used? What did each member of the
team contribute? What resources could you call on to
make sure you move forward or at least take one
more step toward the ideal state? Do you have an
accurate picture in your head of what success or the
ideal looks like? Does the whole team share this

picture? How will you know that you have taken a step forward? What would that look like? What would it feel like? What team learning might need to occur to move toward ten on the scale? Who will take the next step? When will that happen?"

This line of questioning/coaching helps me to think in new ways. It is taken from only one page of this powerful book. I hope that it adds value to your work, coaching, or ministry. I hope that it inspires you to purchase this valuable coaching book.

More Sense of Urgency by John Kotter
(Charlie's Creativity Cast 37. March 17, 2009)

Today's podcast will be another cast based on John Kotter's book titled, "A Sense of Urgency." (Kotter, 2008) If you're following my series, you will have heard cast number twenty seven, which dealt with the four tactics for change. This cast will expand on parts of the earlier one and will form the basis for a presentation to the Presbytery of Donegal on March 21, 2009. Dr. John P. Kotter is the Kenosuke Matsushita Professor of Leadership Emeritus at Harvard Business School. He is widely regarded as the world's foremost authority on leadership and change. He is a well-known author and is especially known for bestsellers such as Leading Change and Our Iceberg is Melting. This book is a powerful, hard hitting quick read on essentials of leading effective change.

Why is it important to discuss leading change and having a sense of urgency? Because we are in an era of massive change! There are many forces swirling around us causing change and disrupting business as usual. We need to find ways of engaging change, adapting the changing circumstances and leading organizations in change.

If you haven't read any of Kotter's books, now is the time. You will find them helpful. Dr. Kotter wrote this book in response to his work and research with organizations trying to change. He saw that the number one problem was creating a sense of urgency in a sufficient number of people to start the ball rolling.

Some organizations can develop hype and get people working harder or going through the motions but it's tougher to get people truly 'on fire' to work with zeal on the critically important areas of business.

Let me share one close at home example in the Presbytery of Donegal. From 2004 to 2008, a period of five years, our overall worship attendance declined by 9%. In that same period, with an average mission budget of about $350,000, we would spend maybe $1500 a year on outreach or evangelism at the presbytery level. Also, we would have great difficulty in getting anyone to serve in the area of evangelism. So, the first important point to emphasize is that leaders need to first make sure that a sufficient number of people feel a true sense of urgency. That there are a sufficient number of people who will work on the organizations critical opportunities and will develop strategies to avoid the hazards and pitfalls. If my memory serves me, Dr. Kotter defines a sufficient number by 10 – 15% of the organization.

The second necessary element is a guiding team that can quickly identify critical issues and then form strong, committed teams around getting things done. These created teams must have a sense of urgency and be composed of the right people – the self-starters. In the military and quality circles, these have sometimes been called, Tiger Teams, a name that has an image of strength and speed.

The third point to emphasize is engaging powerful visions and strategies. By using best in the world strategies and best practices to deal with our critical issues, places us in the upper tier of performers.

The fourth point to stress is the communication piece. Effective, high urgency teams use multiple media and methods to communicate the visions and strategies to the organization with the goal of creating more buy-in and more urgency. One excellent technique that I've learned on the Chestnut Level Presbyterian Church pastor nominating committee is to ask at the end of every meeting, "what in this meeting should be communicated?" Who will do it? What form or medium should be used? When will this be done? These questions are powerful in focusing teams on the importance of communication and using a variety of media to get the information across.

The fifth point is to work on empowerment. Empowerment in this case is speaking about removing obstacles and dealing with the nitty gritty issues that derail efforts. When you've created a high urgency team that is empowered to achieve a vision, they blaze new trails and hack away the brush that hinders progress.

Sixth point. High urgency teams create short term wins to create greater commitment and forward momentum. We all love winning teams, victories and celebrations. By creating bite-sized opportunities to celebrate progress, we visibly gain energy, commitment, and thrust. I've heard of bosses treating staff to donuts and bagels after a special effort to complete a short-term project. Visible, tangible appreciation shows that you notice and you care.

The seventh element is "never letting up." This one flows naturally out of short-term wins in that it calls for a "re-setting" the bar of progress and excellence. After moving forward and achieving mini goals, it is time to standardize and institutionalize these and go from there. When new standards are created, they must be documented, communicated and held as the new baseline process. In this way, the team can continue to climb the mountain toward the vision or goal.

The final element flows naturally from the last one as the true "institutionalizing" piece. The seventh element is about never letting up. Our final element, number eight, is about getting the new processes embedded in the fabric of the institution.

So, there you have a short, quick synopsis of your work as a leader of change.
Create a sense of urgency, gather a core of committed people, tackle critical issues, hold the vision in front of people through communicating, empower your team, celebrate wins, never give up and make it stick. Have a creative week and a sense of urgency!

Collaboration and Decision Making

(Charlie's Creativity Cast 38. March 31, 2009)

Today's cast will be rather short but will be a reflection on the importance of bringing people together for collaboration and decision making. It is the concept of knocking down walls, eliminating stove pipes in organizations and isolated functions. I have seen success in organizations that find ways of bringing many skilled and expert voices to the table for conversation, collaboration and partnering.

Here are examples of this strategy in the Presbytery of Donegal. In the summer of 2005, my boss, the executive presbyter, asked me to take charge of the budgeting process. In previous years, the executive would gather inputs from various committees, work with the bookkeeper and put together a budget. I changed that. I sent out a letter to all of the committee chairs who had budget line items and scheduled a meeting to create a draft budget. We gathered three months before the budget was due to be presented and we hammered out a good draft budget. We then scheduled another meeting a month later to make the budget go final. Everyone loved this process. All were kept informed. All had a voice and a stake in the outcome. All could come to the table and make their case for their financial priorities. This is now the standard, effective process for creating a solid budget. It also creates a sense of camaraderie and buy-in.

Let me tell you about two more recent examples of this strategy. The first is that the presbytery recently received a new church development grant for a Spanish congregation in Lancaster, PA. This congregation is meeting in a very large, very beautiful, but 'expensive to maintain' old church. In order to begin our work, I gathered members of many presbytery committees to give their concerns and inputs. I hosted a meeting with representatives from human resources, property and insurance, finance, new church development, the committee on preparation for ministry, members from the administration department, our business administrator, and the commissioned lay pastor. We brainstormed all our concerns, placed them on sticky notes and then put them on a large board. We grouped them according to categories and then spoke about the issues. By bringing all of these experts together, we built a strong committee team, put faces with names and voices, and positioned this project for a greater chance of success.

Finally, the presbytery is striving to build relationships with our pastors and congregations to help create healthy congregations. Three functions that have a primary role in this are the Committee on Ministry, the Vitalization Division and our Associate for Healthy Congregations. By bringing these three areas together in a collaborative face to face meeting, we've been able to develop a number of powerful new processes. As we discussed our common goals and problems, we were able to build stronger relationships, mutual understandings and commitments for reaching our common aims.

My firm conviction is that, in your own work, as you strive for higher goals and productivity, you will find it effective to knock down walls, eliminate obstacles to communication and get people around tables talking. You'll be very glad you did.

How Do We Fill Our Minds?

(Charlie's Creativity Cast 40. April 25, 2009)

How do we fill our minds? Let me share some personal background with you in order to get into this cast. I come from a solidly churched background and count my blessings as I think about my mother getting four boys ready for church every Sunday and leading the parade down the alley to Trinity United Church of Christ in East Petersburg, PA. I also have fond memories of formal Sunday dinners around by grandparents' table. I believe that at every single meal with my grandpa Truxal, he would ask me what the sermon was about. Well, for a while I would stammer and stutter over that question, for I really could not remember. Then one day the solution came to me. I'd take notes during the sermon so that I could easily summarize it, give the main points or preach it back. This habit of taking notes during sermons has stayed with me ever since. It has expanded to other lectures, presentations and workshops. I think better, stay focused and on point with a journal and a pen. This is and has been a very important discipline for me and a wonderful way to fill my mind.

Another discipline that evolved over time was one of crafting prayers for meals and events in anticipation of being asked. Perhaps because I'm less inhibited than other family members, perhaps because I always say yes, or maybe because God has blessed me in this way, I'm generally asked to say a prayer for a family meal. This was not always easy for me. So, my solution was to start thinking about the meal, the gathering, our thanks-giving, and other related events and experiences long before the meal. What happened was that for many minutes prior to the event, I had been consciously filling my mind with prayers, words, thoughts and blessings for the occasion. Basically, I was praying over and over, playing with words and phrases. Through this mental exercise I became very prepared for the meal prayer and could draw on lots of prayerful words, images and connections. This discipline has blessed me in powerful ways. It keeps me in a prayerful state of mind and allows me to fill my mind with thoughts of the divine and the holy. So, anticipating being called on led me to a prayerful life and a conscious filling my mind with God thoughts.

Another method that I use to fill my mind is with my iPod. I'm a constant student of leadership and process improvement, so I use my iPod to listen to everything I can find on the subject. My twenty-two minutes (and now thirty-nine minutes) on the treadmill every morning provides an excellent chance to work on my body as well as my mind. From either iTunes podcasts or iTunes university, I've heard inspiring and thought-provoking lectures from Harvard IdeaCast, Center for Creative Leadership, Leadership Development from the Banff Centre and hundreds more.

During breakfast, I not only feed my body, but also my mind and soul from God's Word. I'm reading through the Bible again this year at breakfast.

During my travel to the office, my iPod again is plugged in and my virtual university takes to the road. It's awesome to be fed new, creative, stimulating ideas in preparation for my work. The final way I fill my mind is by some reading time in the evening. Well, there you have it. You've heard my story and my routines, so my challenge to you is to examine your interests and your passions and assess how you fill your minds. I'd love to hear of your creative ideas.

Presbyterian Leadership Concepts
(Charlie's Creativity Cast 42. May 25, 2009)

This cast will share information from a short booklet published in March 2009 by Elder Linda Valentine and the Rev. Dr. Clifton Kirkpatrick, titled, Presbyterian Leadership, Reflections on Leadership Renewal in the Presbyterian Church U.S.A. The premise is that we need bold, creative, innovative leadership in the church to move us into the future God intends for us. The other claim is that our seminaries are not preparing women and men in the skills necessary to transform the church. This gap in abilities creates a wonderful opportunity for a college of leadership or a leadership laboratory initiative. I challenge you to consider that and would love to join that conversation. But I digress.

The booklet highlights five characteristics of Presbyterian leadership. I will list them, then speak briefly about each one. The five are: shared leadership, seeks transformation, grounded in holistic vision, modeled on Jesus Christ, and honors diversity.

The characteristic of shared leadership is central to our Presbyterian polity. We hold strongly to the belief that we come together as elders, both ruling elders and teaching elders (Ministers of Word and Sacrament) as equals in the assembly to lead God's people by discerning the will of Christ. Calvin established a system of shared power in Geneva between the consistory and the company of pastors. In our reformed tradition, we value the "priesthood of all believers." As we share leadership, it behooves us to both "bring out the best" in one another and to also find ways to support and strengthen one another. As we share and care, we will use spiritual disciplines and practices to share joys, concerns, ideas and encouragement.

The second characteristic is that leadership is about transformation. Going back to our Calvin roots, we know that Calvin made it clear in his doctrine of sanctification that the reason we have been saved is to live our life to the glory of God and to share in God's project of transforming the world. We are to live in such a way that we model the reign of God, where all can live together in peace, justice, and community in right relationship to God. And so our task as a leader is to work toward transformative, faithful change. Jesus challenged nearly everyone he met to do something and change. Turn, repent, change your heart, change your attitude, change your inward focus. And so as we are reformed and always being reformed, we are to lead the way.

The third characteristic is a holistic vision. Inspiring vision is a core principle of leadership. Leaders are to encourage, challenge and bring out the best in communities of people as they proclaim the good news of Jesus Christ, uphold the truth, worship God, seek justice and walk the walk and talk the talk. Leaders relentlessly paint the picture of the future, help people imagine it, and emphasize the shared core values and mission of God.

The fourth characteristic for leaders is that their source and model for life is Jesus Christ. The ultimate leader in our life is Jesus Christ. So our role as a leader is to point people to Jesus and his way in the world. Of course, the other side of this premise is that as a leader, we need to be rooted deeply in prayer, scripture and our walk with the Lord. When we solidify our personal relationship with Christ, we are more able to point others to this truth, way and life. One of the greatest sermons Jesus ever preached was in the upper room when he took a towel and the role of the lowest slave and served his disciples, his friends. He modeled servant leadership by doing it. Not by talking about it or studying it, but by actually doing it.

The fifth and final characteristic lifted up is "effective leadership honors diversity and reaches out to the world." This trait again is modeled by our savior as he was committed to diversity and inclusiveness in age, gender and culture. This is stated in Galatians 3:28 by the Apostle Paul. "There is neither Jew nor Greek, slave nor free, male nor female, but all are one in Christ." Our role as leaders is to bring all people and voices together and empower communities of diverse gifts. Practice being welcoming and using extravagant hospitality. Struggle to understand "the other" as they seek to glorify God.

Friends, we have a very rich heritage as Presbyterians, let us strive tirelessly to equip, encourage and empower leaders for the future. I am grateful for the Board of Pensions who printed and distributed this booklet. May God Richly Bless you as you take up your yoke of leadership.

Some concepts from "What Would Google Do?"

(Charlie's Creativity Cast 43. June 6, 2009)

Today I want to reflect on or ramble about our personal or corporate intersection with the world and culture. A good friend of mine, Kris Gerling, referred me to the Jeff Jarvis book titled, "What Would Google Do?" (Jarvis, 2009) I am half way through it and it has some fascinating concepts about continual learning. Google learns from every click of the mouse. Google is an incredible innovator in terms of services and tools – constantly learning, constantly experimenting and constantly trying things out. In fact, if you use Google, you will notice that it is always in "beta" testing. This behemoth, wildly successful company tracks trends and movements of cultures. They provide tools for bringing people together, linking ideas, interests, and markets. They profit by connecting sellers and buyers through ads.

The question to ponder is this: "Do they influence, flavor or leaven the culture with their tools

or do they simply make cultural movements easier?"
The reason that I would like to explore this has to do
with my work in the Presbyterian Church. I wonder
how we can become more of an influence on our
culture because of the Holy Spirit living in us, rather
than being those whom simply ride the tide of the
world. I wonder how we might be as innovative,
creative and bold to leaven the culture with our hope
found in Jesus Christ. We have rich, deep, glorious,
long-standing traditions, but as we look and see the
blinding speed of change that swirls around us, we
need to be re-tooled, equipped and sent out to boast
in the one who is God with us.   Immanuel, Jesus
Christ. There is an excellent statement in the Jarvis
book that says that companies want to start new
conversation communities to try to move them toward
their products. The counter wisdom is that there are
already communities of people gathering, working,
playing, doing things that benefit the world. The tact
for companies and also for the church is to go beyond
our walls and to join those people, to BE the church

and to BE God's people in the world. Perhaps our greatest need is for practical laboratories or test ranges to practice connecting our faith with real life in the world. How do we practice being the church in the world when we mostly practice being the church in the church? I have heard of churches having holy conversations in bars, going into the community to clean up, and planting gardens to feed those who need some help. What are other ways we could do "beta" testing on bringing the Spirit of Immanuel, God with us to the world that needs it so badly? I would love to hear your ideas.

More on "What Would Google Do?"
(Charlie's Creativity Cast 44. June 20, 2009)

This cast will be a part two on the Jeff Jarvis book, "What Would Google Do?" (Jarvis, 2009) But, it will be a mash-up with my work in the Presbyterian Church. I will explore some intersections of ideas.

One of the main points in the book is to decide what business you're in. As Presbyterians, followers of Jesus Christ, we are in the business of worshiping the Sovereign, Holy, Almighty God. We are people who place our full hope, trust and future on God as revealed in Jesus Christ, God's Son, the living Word. We are people who are sent by God into the world, led by the Holy Spirit and guided by the Written Word, the Bible. So, if that is at least an elementary attempt at our business definition, then what's next? Well Mr. Jarvis says that an effective strategy is to fixate on our customer, produce an excellent product or service, and provide outstanding customer service. It seems to me that this means our focus is on meeting people in their needs – being in the world and in our communities in ways that assist, bless and care for God's people. We must find innovative ways to give ourselves away and empty ourselves for others. And, in this selfless service, we do it all with excellence, love and humility. And if, when serving we are asked, we explain that we are in the service of the Sovereign, Holy God who loves us and wants the best for us. We explain that we cannot do less, because we are sent to work for healing, for reconciliation, for justice, for wholeness and for peace in the world.

I believe that as we worship and serve Almighty God, we will joyfully be turned inside out. We will focus more on those beyond our walls – those who don't know the joy of Jesus Christ. We will focus on the abundance that comes from worshiping the creator of the universe and then will be sent to bless those around us.

Well, these are only a couple of the points made in this interesting book. You would benefit from he read as you could explore the topics of distributed conversations collaboration and giving away control.

Reviewing "Humble Leadership"

(Charlie's Creativity Cast 45. July 3, 2009)

I've just finished Graham Standish's book titled, Humble Leadership, Being Radically Open to God's Guidance and Grace. It's a very worthwhile book to add to your library. Let me tell you why.

Graham speaks eloquently of the virtue of humility in prayerfully seeking God's will, voice and direction. He says, and I quote, "Humility is a way of life in which we become consumed with seeking God's direction rather than living purely according to our instincts, conditioning and insights." (Standish, 2007) Then, our leadership is about leading others with that openness to God. The book stresses laying down our will and picking up the will of God for all things. The author criticizes us as being closed to God. He says that the mainline church today suffers from a crisis of creativity. We too infrequently ask the critical question, "What is God's will?" We limit our leadership, opportunities and possibilities by using

151

worldly wisdom in our decision making and leadership. By using worldly standards, we close out the miracles that are totally in the realm of Almighty God! One chapter of the book helps us examine our leadership styles and stresses "self-aware" leadership. Graham believes that it is important to use counseling and spiritual direction to help us gain personal awareness around our leadership issues. He says that the more aware we are of ourselves, the more our ministry has the potential of being Christ's ministry – rooted in God's purpose and empowered by the Holy Spirit.

Another chapter of the book emphasizes the importance of prayerful leadership. A leader who humbles herself in prayer leads faithfully and well. Leadership rooted in a relationship with the creator requires time spent listening to God. Rev. Standish cites the Acts 2:42 passage as a powerful model for Christian leadership. It states, "They devoted themselves to the apostles' teaching, and fellowship, to the breaking of bread and the prayers." For humble, faithful, powerful and effective leadership, prayer is central. For busy people and pastors, this life-giving discipline is easily put aside for other activities. It may be time to stop and examine this aspect of our lives and then schedule prayer, put it on our calendars, seek out times and places to pray and make it a priority.

I know that this is a short glimpse into some very powerful advice. My follow-on advice is to read the book and even, more importantly, I recommend the application of Graham Standish's advice! Until next time, have a creative, prayerful week!

Leadership Development Strategy

(Charlie's Creativity Cast 46. July 16, 2009)

I appreciate your time and engagement with me on some vital leadership issues. Today's cast lays down a challenge for you. I think that, as a subscriber to this creativity podcast series, you're the type to answer the challenge. So, let me give you some brief musings on the background of the challenge and then I'll lay it out for you.

I've been reading a fascinating book by Tony Morgan titled, Killing Cockroaches and Other Musings on Leadership. (Morgan, 2009) Tony is the chief strategic officer at Newspring Church in Anderson, South Carolina. Tony is a great thinker, an avid blogger and can be read at TonyMorganLive.com. He has stirred up my mental pot and is creating a thoughtful stew on the topic of future leadership. If you've listened to this series before, you know that I have an unquenchable desire to learn, so I search iTunes and iTunesU for e-books, podcasts, courses and lectures on leadership, coaching, innovation and creativity. Of course, I also love bookstores, google, good search, and other large databases of educational resources, and frequently search for new experiences.

I'm slowly getting into using social networking tools like Facebook and Twitter and realize the interactive power of holding virtual discussions. Based on Tony Morgan's inspiration, I'm thinking that I should be doing more blogging. The point is, at the moment, I'm doing a self-directed almost random scan for leadership development resources and experiences. So, here's my question about resources, experiences, conversation partners, mission trips, lectures, small groups, books, podcasts, videos and life. Is my process of self-focused learning and scanning an efficient way of designing my leadership preparation for God's marvelous but uncertain future? I'm curious to know if my process of undirected searching is adequate or if there is a better way. Creating a reading list, a course plan or a focused curriculum seems like a technical fix for leadership development and seems to be bounded by more linear assumptions and the past, than on an adaptive solution. Perhaps following a PhD track or other guided mentor could streamline my efforts, so I'm very curious. I'm wondering what new ideas, roles or situations are optimal for preparing leaders for the future. Maybe I'm just searching for conversation partners on this work. Specifically, I'd like to explore preparing ministry leaders for the future. So, the challenge to you is this: Design a process, a position description, a set of skills, a set of experiences, a reading list, courses to take, places to go, people to meet, things to see and do that will prepare leaders for the future in the church. Perhaps you could create an interactive database or host a dynamic discussion on this topic. In doing this, it will be helpful to name your key assumptions and desired outcomes. Or, said in a different way, as we develop ministry leaders, what is your starting point? What will be the traits, behaviors and characteristics of leaders who

undertake your process? This will be a valuable use
of your time and I'd love to get that type of feedback.
Have a great week!

Ideas from the Global Leadership Summit
(Charlie's Creativity Cast 48. August 8, 2009)

As I write this podcast, I am in the middle of the Willow Creek Global Leadership Summit. I am experiencing God's extravagant blessings through a powerhouse of speakers, interviews, round tables, videos, prayers and worship. From Bill Hybels' opening entitled, "Leading in a new reality," where he likened our economic situation to a rogue wave of 80 feet in height, he urged leaders to speak into the current reality and to help the church live out the Acts 2 community in the current day. This calls us to step up our faith, step up our serving, step-up our praying, our giving and leading the church to be the church for the world.

One of the world's leading strategists, Gary Hamel, gave some hard-hitting advice. He urged us to conquer denial by facing facts, being real with everyone, questioning our assumptions and listening to the renegade/fringe voices. He also urged us to generate more strategic options, which equates to doing more super brainstorming, wherein there are no bad ideas and no pre-judging ideas. He chided us to do create "ideastorms" like Dell and not rush to closure on these ideas. Another thought that Gary shared was to "deconstruct orthodoxy." He said that we need new ideas, innovation and creativity to mash together BIG ideas. We need to create open space, divergent processes, wide participation and courage to risk and dream. Gary says that the leader's job is to mobilize, connect and support. Leaders need to build more flexible, dynamic, malleable organizations that can capture the power from the people and make a tangible difference in the world.

Later we heard from Jessica Jackley, the creator of an incredible micro finance company that is now connecting donors like you and me to entrepreneurial recipients across the globe. According to Jessica, it's very simple. She has partnered with a large number of other micro finance institutions to qualify the recipients, so by going to

KIVA.org, you can search for a person or situation to whom you can make a $25, $50, $100 loan. The success rate is averaging around 98.5%, so only a few default on the loan. She is helping to connect people to people and she is changing the world. You can join her by going to KIVA.ORG and making a loan.

We also heard the Rev. Harvey Carey, a high energy preacher from Detroit, on how God is moving his church beyond their walls. God's people are shutting down crack houses and are literally cleaning up the poorest zip code of this city. He tells us to stop just huddling on Sunday mornings and get out and do something for the kingdom. We are called to be the church of Jesus Christ in the world. Not just on Sunday mornings in our historic buildings, but wherever we go.

We met Andrew Rugasira, a native of Kampala, Uganda, whose company is called, "Good African Coffee," but whose mission is to deconstruct the negative image of the continent of Africa. His premise is that in Africa, there are 53 countries with around 900 million potential entrepreneurs who know how to live on $1/day. To change this continent, we need to find ways to trade with them rather than giving them aid. Andrew challenges us to look for the opportunities and not the negative perceptions and images. He also asked us to buy African shirts, teas, and coffee and help change the tide of their confidence and self-esteem.

I can't summarize all the excellence that I experienced in these two days, but I do prioritize this event in my leadership development plan and strongly suggest that you add this to your calendar, too. It is generally held during the first week of August. In 2010, it is scheduled for August 5 and 6. Well, I'm off to reflect on what I heard, then integrate it into my life and finally, pray for God's guidance to revolutionize this world.

The Future of Management Part One
(Charlie's Creativity Cast 49. August 24, 2009)

This cast was inspired by attending the Willow
Creek Global Leadership Summit in August 2009. I
heard Gary Hamel, a world renown strategist and
London Business School professor speak. I then
purchased and started reading his book, titled, "The
Future of Management," which he co-authored with
Bill Breen. (Hamel, 2007) I could not put the book
down. I bought it on Friday night and by Sunday
afternoon was halfway through it. Here's why:

Gary makes a strong case for us to ask hard
questions about the way we organize, plan,
implement and carry out work. He calls us to be
innovators and innovators are never bound by what
is. They dream of what could be. The book's goal is
to help us imagine and then create the future of
management. Perhaps one of the reasons that I am
glued to this book is that Gary is urging leaders to
acquire a passion for solving extraordinary problems,

daunting problems, problems which would fuel the imagination, creativity and energy. He encourages a bold passion which elevates our collaboration and our thinking and draws us into energetic communities.

The following are some of the questions we are asked to consider: What are the new challenges for your organization? What are the "tomorrow" problems that should be worked on today? What are the tough balancing issues you are facing? What are the either/or tradeoffs that need to be dealt with? What are the biggest gaps between rhetoric and reality? How do you make what you believe and say become what you really do? Finally, what are you indignant about? What are the frustrating incompetency's that plaque your organization? What is deemed impossible that has to become possible? These are huge questions and are posed to stir our hearts and brains. They are laid out to help us get out of our comfortable routines. They serve as a challenge to pull together the organization to work on tomorrow's problems. Facing the future reality today and intentionally laying groundwork, building capacity, learning new ways to interact and building strong community relationships.

To face reality together takes courage and trust among the individuals of the organization. Working to change rhetoric into reality is hard work and takes time. These are all leadership challenges that are worthy of our time and effort. My goal is to translate these questions for the Presbytery of Donegal and then face the future challenges by setting bold goals, by building community and capacity, by seeking God's wisdom and by loving God's people. I am exceedingly thankful for the future-oriented thinking of Bill Hybels and for the challenging, thought-provoking work of Gary Hamel and Bill Breen.

Developing Innovative Management Practices
(Charlie's Creativity Cast 50. August 30, 2009)

Thank-you for joining me in this 50th podcast in my creativity series. What a neat milestone. I started these in January 2008 and have averaged a cast every 12 days. Before I dive into my topic for today, I have to promote an amazingly informative and fun podcast. It is called, Leadership Starts Here. The author is Jeff Newland from Rochester, NY. In August 2009, Jeff was the executive director of Big Brothers and Big Sisters in Rochester. He has since that time changed agencies, but his excellent series of podcasts are informative, entertaining and humorous. Check him out on iTunes.

Today's cast will cover a few more reflections from the Gary Hamel and Bill Breen book titled, "The Future of Management." (Hamel, 2007) According to the authors, the goal of the book is to be a catalyst for us to create new innovations in management. The authors make some helpful observations of current large company creativity, then ask the readers some powerful, focused questions to be applied to their own contexts.

Here's what I took away from this excellent management springboard: One of the best ways to discover effective leadership practices is to conduct a large number of management experiments. Be bold. Lead. Try something and learn. Decentralize decision making and find ways to give employees ownership and a stake in the results. Create a democracy of ideas and a free market economy on innovations. Work on new ways of incentivizing employee ideas and contributions. Make liberal use of the internet or company intranet. Open up and be very transparent with ideas, decisions and your management style. Talk about the need for creativity and innovative solutions all the time and then give people freedom to innovate and experiment in their own work. Ask colleagues some of these radical questions: What difference do we make in the world? What goals should we go for that would require personal risk and adventure? What accomplishments could we achieve that would be revolutionary or breath-taking? What do we want to tell our children or grandchildren we did?

I don't know how these ideas hit you, but they energize me and give me a boost in enthusiasm. They remind me that we have all been gifted in unique ways and wise leaders work to bring out the best in employees. Hamel and Breen believe that some of our most important work is creating innovative management practices for the 21st century and developing capable leaders for the future. I'd like to take them up on the challenge. How about you?

Planting Seeds that Bear Fruit

(Charlie's Creativity Cast 51. September 12, 2009)

I consider my three years of being the acting Executive Presbyter for Donegal as a "post-graduate level" course. It has stretched me and blessed me in amazing ways. On Tuesday, September 15, 2009, we will be voting on calling a new Executive Presbyter. I am thrilled and enthusiastic about working with this talented, passionate servant of God.

But now, I have a story to tell you. It's a story of seed planting that is bearing fruit. It's a story that originates in the thinking and communicating of the Rev. Dr. Michael Wilson. Here it is: In 2007, Chestnut Level Presbyterian Church was beginning a capital campaign to build a three-million-dollar family life center. In the planning for this, Michael told me that this project had the potential to be focused inward and be all about raising money for themselves. To help counter this inward focus and balance out this tendency, he purposely and intentionally added various outward looking components. They stressed the outward reach to the community and also conducted Bible studies to look outward to the world's needs. He told me about this balancing strategy and planted a very important seed in my brain. I carried that seed around and it dawned on me that the Presbytery of Donegal was going into a season of studying itself through the use of a transition consultant, a transition team, and a plethora of holy conversations. This had the potential to be all about us. All about the Presbytery of Donegal. On a beautiful summer evening, my wife and I were invited to a dinner at the home of the Rev. Jim and Lois Caldwell. The Caldwells are nationally known mission consultants and are passionate in their love for and service to Jesus Christ. Well, at dinner, the seed that Michael planted started to grow. I mentioned my concern for the potential inward focus of our transition year and asked how we could propose a year of mission to the Presbytery Council and to the presbytery. Within a few weeks we settled on a proposal for "The Year of World Mission." With that title and theme, the Caldwells laid out an incredibly rich matrix of speakers, events, and experiences that focused the presbytery on God's global mission and our connection to that mission. The seed was growing into a healthy, living tree of life. 2008 was a powerful year of world mission. In fact, this seed had produced a plant so healthy that it was about to yield early fruit. A wonderful couple (and for security reasons, I can't say their names) from one of our large Chester County churches were starting to feel God's nudge toward the mission field. When they heard of our year's focus and saw the power and importance of God's global mission, they knew in their hearts that this was their calling. They are now settled in the mission field as Presbyterian Church U.S.A. mission co-workers and are bearing more global fruit. Since that time, two more mission co-workers, the Rev. Larry and Barb Moir, have been sent by our presbytery into the mission field. Of the

225 PC(USA) mission co-workers, Donegal has seven. That is over five times the expected average.

You see my friends, the seeds that you plant can and do bear fruit that you cannot even know. Thank-you Michael for sharing your ideas and planting those seeds! It may be an overused image, but you can count the number of seeds in an apple, but you cannot count the number of apples in a seed. Friends who serve Jesus, keep sharing your faith and hope and keep planting those seeds. You'll never know how God will produce fruit from your seeds.

Intentional Community and Conversations

(Charlie's Creativity Cast 54. November 1, 2009)

I would like to reflect for a third time on the Gary Hamel and Bill Breen book, The Future of Management. (Hamel, 2007) I was reviewing my notes on my Kindle and just get so energized and encouraged by the notes made on this book.

One of the over-riding themes of this book is the building of capacity and creativity by building community. Community is formed by creating an environment of trust and respect and the built-in expectation that all will contribute to, not only the organizational mission, but to the everyday improvements toward that mission.

According to Hamel and Breen, jobs of the future are all about experimentation, innovation, learning how to create and add value and how to enhance that each and every day. The authors suggest setting aside fifteen to twenty minutes in meetings to build community and capacity by asking questions like, "What difference do we want to make in the world? What will our business look like in five to ten years? What are we willing to 'go for' or take risks for? How can we innovate? What are we willing to work tirelessly to accomplish? What do we want to tell our kids or grandkids we did for society or the world?" (Hamel, 2007)

To survive in tomorrow's economy, we need to be intentional about crafting conversations that create synergistic communities. We need to create management styles that are unconventionally competitive. By rewarding learning, experimentation and innovation, we will have the best chance of producing an excellent, value producing, competitive organization. How shall we begin this? By being intentional in our conversations, intentional with new meeting agendas, intentional with new position descriptions, intentional with new expectations and new questions. We also begin by asking our employees to innovate, experiment and try new approaches to solve our problems. I think that I'm going to start this week. What will you do with this information?

The Clean Sweep Produces Energy and Vitality

(Charlie's Creativity Cast 55. November 10, 2009)

I am honored that you've chosen to spend this much time with me. I started writing this particular podcast on November 10, 2009. November 10th is a very special day in my life. That day, thirty years ago at Williams Air Force Base, near Phoenix, Arizona, a beautiful little girl came into this world. We named her Angela Sue. I'm very proud of her, her hard work, her care and compassion as a mom and wife, her roofing ability in Hurricane Katrina relief, and finally her devotion to a goal of becoming a Registered Nurse. She achieved this in September 2009 after six long years of part time studies. This cast is dedicated to my beautiful daughter, Angie.

Hey, thanks for waiting for me. I've been travelling and vacationing in October 2009, for most of the month. Then, for the last week or so, I've been catching up and getting ready for the dynamic future! I certainly appreciate your patience. Maybe in a future cast I'll tell you about my vacation, but this one will give you a super energy producing shot in the arm. (Well, this advice worked for me) Here goes.

I am doing some research on pursuing a certification as a life coach or as an executive coach. One potential school of coaching that I'm investigating is called, CoachU Inc. You can find it on the web at: www.coachinc.com. It is accredited by the International Coach Federation. In their handbook called, "Becoming a Coach," by Sandy Vilas, there is a section called the Clean Sweep Program. This is a program developed by the staff, trainers and participants of Coach U, Inc. It is a one hundred item checklist designed to give you a healthy and vital lifestyle. It's designed to give you energy and momentum in life. The program consists of four major areas with twenty-five checklist items in each area. The four major areas are: physical environment, health and emotional balance, money, and relationships. Here is why I am excited to tell you about this. I recently did only a few hours work on my

physical environment and I got really pumped up! I
spent some time cleaning out my closet, clearing it of
pants and shirts that I no longer wear. Then I
organized my top dresser drawer. These two items fit
into just two of the twenty-five items in the physical
environment area, so I am only just beginning. But I
have to tell you, the energy that those two things
produced, simply amazed me. My clothes aren't all
jammed in my closet and my dresser looks good. I
feel better from this minor cleaning job. Oh, you know
what happened next? A few days later, I went
through my office desk drawers and organized them.
I'm on an organizational roll and it's like a snowball
rolling downhill.   It's picking up speed, gaining energy
and reinforcing itself.

Here's the takeaway. If you want to produce
more energy and vitality in your life, start to simplify it
and declutter it. Throw stuff away, give stuff away,
store stuff elsewhere, and organize your living space
and your workspace. It will give you more energy and
more vitality. The Japanese have an excellent quality

program, called the five S's, that assists you in this.
I'll tell you about the five S's in the next podcast. Until
then, have a great organizing week.

The 5 S's of housekeeping by Masaaki Imai

(Charlie's Creativity Cast 56. November 17, 2009)

Welcome to my creativity podcast. In the last cast, I told you about the energy I got from simply clearing out a closet and cleaning up my dresser. It reminded me of a great book I read in the late 1990's called, Gemba Kaizen – A commonsense, low cost approach to management by Masaaki Imai. The book is full of down to earth advice on productivity, and efficiency techniques. I'll only briefly cover the 5 S's.

The 5 S's stand for five Japanese words, but I'll use the English equivalents. They are Sort, Straighten, Scrub, Systematize and Standardize. These form the basis of nearly any work operation or office situation. It is basic housekeeping. Here's how it works: The first S is for Sort. It means to separate out all that is unnecessary in your work environment and eliminate it. If you examine your work area, you can sort and separate your materials into two groups – necessary and unnecessary. The rule suggested by the author is to remove anything that will not be used within the next 30 days. Excess supplies and materials should be stored elsewhere AND restocking levels should be determined so that only a small amount of inventory is maintained.

The second S is Straighten. This step gets us to place all of our tools within easy reach. Place your pen, paper, CDs, DVDs, and files within arm's reach to eliminate unnecessary motion. Also, have only the incoming material in your space that you can process. It's efficient to limit the flow to your desk and it keeps your area organized.

The third S is for Scrub. This may be more important in a manufacturing environment than an office situation, but having a clean, dust free environment is healthier and more pleasant. Make sure that there is a regular routine of cleaning, dusting, and sweeping.

The fourth S is for Systematize. This requires a discipline of following a process of accomplishing work and then returning the tools to their location. By having a good working system, you can guarantee a high-quality output.

The fifth and last S is for Standardize. It can also mean self-discipline. By creating a constantly improving standardized way of working, you can create a continuously improving result. Each time an improvement is made and then standardized; the quality bar is raised.

So, there you have the ground floor of a quality management initiative and an improved working environment. By sorting, straightening, scrubbing, systematizing, and standardizing your work and your work area, you are poised to tackle more serious improvement projects.

Put Some Hot Sauce in your Espresso!

(Charlie's Creativity Cast 61. January 3, 2010)

Put some hot sauce in your espresso! I've had this crazy idea for a few weeks now, maybe a few months. I have an image of myself as being creative, innovative, one who is gifted by God with a vivid, active imagination. So, I often get abstract, zany, off the wall ideas. I don't know which causes what. Does myself image produce this outcome or do I get these, "push the envelope" ideas which causes my self-image? Oh, my name is Charlie Gross. Welcome to my podcast series. Anyway, here's my idea for you for this year. Put some hot sauce in your espresso! That's it. That's the image. And, actually, it's Sunday morning, January 3, 2010 and partially to warm up, I've brewed my second cup of Papa Nicholas espresso in my old Krups espresso maker, and I put a healthy dose of Louisiana hot sauce in it. It hasn't added to the flavor. It's not terrible or anything, but I think it's more of an image or metaphor that captured me. I mean, just last night with some good friends, we watched an episode of Cirque du Sole. Mind boggling precision, timing, strength and creativity on a big stage. I mean perfection and excellence! Awe inspiring performance. I wanted to clap with the audience. I don't know why I didn't. Actually, at the very end, I did a light applause.

Now I don't imagine that the disciplined athletes in Cirque du Sole put hot sauce in their espresso, but their sense of going for it, pushing the limits in their own bodies inspires me to do more, encourage more, dream more, and strive harder for perfection, excellence, and top notch performance.

As I get closer to the bottom of my espresso, I realize that the hot sauce was heavier than the coffee. It has an interesting kick to it. I'm not convinced that this will be my morning routine, but the image is a keeper. I hope and pray that this year will be one that I add superior value to my family, my ministry, my friends, and God's fabulous creation. I'd love it if you joined me in this work. Visit me at

www.charliegross.com or send your comments to
cwgross@gmail.com. Oh, and if do put hot sauce in
your espresso, watch out for the last sip! Have a
great creative week! Bye for now.

Bibliography

Bennis, W. (2003). *On Becoming A Leader.* New York: Basic Books.

Bersin, J. (2008). Leadership Development in 2008. *Chief Learning Officer*, 18.

Clutterbuck, D. (2007). *Coaching the Team at Work.* New York: Nicholas Brealey Publishing.

Friedman, S. (2008). *Total Leadership.* New York: HB Press.

Hamel, G. B. (2007). *The Future of Management.* New York: Harvard Business School Press.

Hargrove, R. (2003). *Masterful Coaching.* New York: John Wiley and Sons.

Jarvis, J. (2009). *What Would Google Do?* New York: HarperCollins.

Kegan, R. a. (2001). *How the Way We Talk Can Change the Way We Work.* New York: Wiley.

185

Kotter, J. (2008). *A Sense of Urgency*. New York:
    Harvard Business Press.

Lencioni, P. (2002). *The Five Dysfunctions of a Team.*
    New York: Jossey-Bass.

Miller, K. A. (2004). *Surviving Information Overload.*
    New York: Zondervan.

Morgan, T. (2009). *Killing Cockroaches.* Nashville,
    Tennessee: B&H Publishing Group.

Patterson, K., Grenny, J., Maxfield, D., McMillan, R.,
    & Switzler, A. (2002). *Crucial Conversations -
    Tools for talking when stakes are high*. New
    York: McGraw-Hill.

Patterson, K., Grenny, J., Maxfield, D., McMillan, R.,
    & Switzler, A. (2005). *Crucial Confrontations -
    Tools for resolving broken promises, violated
    expectations and bad behavior*. New York:
    McGraw-Hill.

Patterson, K., Grenny, J., Maxfield, D., McMillan, R., & Switzler, A. (2008). *Influencer - The Power to Change Anything.* New York: McGraw-Hill.

Peters, T. (2006). *Re-Imagine! Business Excellence in a Disruptive Age.* New York: DK Adult.

Pink, D. H. (2005). *A Whole New Mind: Why Right-Brainers will Rule the Future.* New York: Riverhead.

Senge, P. S. (2004). *Presence: An Exploration of Profound Change in People, Organizations, and Society.* New York: Doubleday.

Standish, N. G. (2007). *Humble Leadership.* Herndon, Virginia: The Alban Institute.

Tichy, N. M. (1997). *The Leadership Engine: How Winning Companies Build Leaders at Every Level.* New York: Harper Business.

Wheatley, M. (2009). *Turning To One Another: Simple Conversations to Restore Hope to the Future.* New York: Berrett Koehler Publishers.

Whitworth, K.-H. S. (2007). *Co-Active Coaching.* New York: Davies-Black Publishing.

Zander, R. S., & Zander, B. (2000). *The Art of Possibility: Transforming Your Professional and Personal Life.* New York: Penquin Books.